Developing

Consideration,

Respect

and Tolerance

Karen Brunskill

P·CP
Paul Chapman
Publishing

A Lucky Duck Book

Paul Chapman Publishing
A SAGE Publications Company
1 Oliver's Yard
55 City Road
London EC1Y 1SP

SAGE Publications Inc.
2455 Teller Road
Thousand Oaks, California 91320

SAGE Publications India Pvt Ltd.
B-42, Panchsheel Enclave
Post Box 4109
New Delhi 110 017

www.luckyduck.co.uk

Commissioning Editor: George Robinson
Editorial Team: Mel Maines, Sarah Lynch, Wendy Ogden
Designer: Nick Shearn
Illustrations: Leanne Winfield, Katie Jardine, Helen Sylvester, Michael Dell, Lori Head, Claire Saxby, Jacquie Young, Helen Miles, Ian Moule, Jennifer Cooke

A catalogue record for this book is available from the British Library
Library of Congress Control Number 2006900193

ISBN13 978-1-4129-1963-0
ISBN10 1-4129-1963-0

Printed on paper from sustainable resources
Printed in Great Britain by The Cromwell Press Ltd, Trowbridge, Wiltshire

The CD-ROM contains PDF files labelled 'Worksheets.pdf' which consists of the stories and worksheets for each unit in this resource. You will need Acrobat Reader version 3 or higher to view and print these resources.

The documents are set up to print to A4 but you can enlarge them to A3 by increasing the output percentage at the point of printing using the page set-up settings for your printer.

Contents

The *Promoting Children's Resilience and Wellbeing* series were originally published in Australia as the *Values for Life* series of books, and when we saw them we felt they would provide valuable additions to our range of books on emotional literacy. One of the attractions was that the four books provided a coherent programme from early years through to 12.

Book 1: *Learning to be Honest, Kind and Friendly* (Age range: 5 to 7)

Book 2: *Learning to be Confident, Determined and Caring* (Age range: 5 to 7)

Book 3: *Developing Consideration, Respect and Tolerance* (Age range: 7 to 9)

Book 4: *Enhancing Courage, Respect and Assertiveness* (Age range: 9 to 12)

In Australia the term 'emotional resilience' is more widely used than in the UK, though the term is increasingly current here. Resilience is the ability to recover from adversity or difficult situations or circumstances. Fuller (2001) suggests that life events are 'contagious'. Life events, both positive and negative, establish chains of behaviour. If children are faced with negative events their interpretation of these events will influence how they cope. If they don't have resilience they are likely to react in a negative way.

An example of a negative or risk chain would be:

> a child who grows up in violent circumstances and learns to distrust others, enters school and interprets the intention of others as hostile. The child then acts warily or aggressively towards peers and develops peer relationship problems...

An example of a positive or protective chain would be:

> a child who grows up in violent circumstances but learns, on entry to school, that there is a trustworthy adult who can be relied on to assist in the resolution of peer relationship difficulties. The child's positive attempts to interact with others are acknowledged. The child begins to feel accepted, mixes more appropriately with peers and develops a diversity of friendships. (Fuller, 2001)

The work of Goleman (1995) indicates that the promotion of protective factors in school life is not only predictive of academic success but even more importantly for positive adult life outcomes.

The idea of positive factors that promote resilience has been supported by research (Resnick, Harris and Blum, 1993; Fuller, McGraw and Goodyear, 1998). The main factors appear to be:

▶ family connectedness

▶ peer connectedness

▶ fitting in at school.

Two of these can be directly influenced by school life, creating positive experiences that are 'contagious'.

Resilience seems to depend largely on this sense of belonging. Once one belongs, empathy can develop and empathy builds group cohesion where moral actions such as honesty, altruism and caring emerge developmentally as the child matures.

This idea of resilience can be seen to be important in all areas of school life, as quoted in Fuller (2001):

> When schools promote belonging and ensure high levels of involvement between staff and students, bullying is reduced. (Citing the work of Olweus, 1995; Rigby 1996.)

This series, with its progressive programme, allows the opportunity for young people to explore:

▸ consideration	▸ courage	▸ tolerance
▸ honesty	▸ caring	▸ respect
▸ responsibility	▸ friendliness	▸ determination
▸ confidence	▸ kindness	▸ assertiveness.

As children mature the level that these can be explored becomes deeper; their reasoning and morality becomes more sophisticated with age and this type of programme can assist in their 'connectedness'. Our increasing awareness of the concept of 'Citizenship' should recognise elements such as empathy, moral reasoning and moral behaviour.

Current UK initiatives

The Healthy Schools Programme identifies emotional health and wellbeing (including bullying) as one of the areas schools have to develop and are required to produce evidence that they have met the necessary criteria. The Healthy Schools Programme, of course, is not a separate entity divorced from all other aspects of school development. The statutory components of PSHE and Citizenship for primary schools can be linked to the concept of emotional health and wellbeing and, we would also argue, emotional resilience.

The 12 domains covered in this programme fit the four components of PSHE and Citizenship at Key Stage 1 and 2:

1. Developing confidence and responsibility and making the most of their abilities.

2. Preparing to play an active role as citizens.

3. Developing a healthy, safer lifestyle.

4. Developing good relationships and respecting the difference between people.

The introduction of developing children's social, emotional and behavioural skills (SEBS) also highlights the importance of the type of material presented in this book.

▸ Emotional and social competence have been shown to be more influential than cognitive abilities for personal, career and scholastic success.

▸ Programmes that teach social and emotional competences have been shown to result in a wide range of educational gains.

▸ Work and workplace increasingly focus on social and emotional competences with increased emphasis on teamwork, communication, management skills etc. (DfES, 2003)

Though resilience is not mentioned directly, SEBS clearly identifies the earlier point about the 'contagious' effects of life events.

> Research is bringing home the wide extent of various types of neglect and abuse. This is being exacerbated by the breakdown of extended family and communities which reduces support for the nuclear family, and the higher rates of divorce and subsequent one-parent families. This has led to a shake-up in belief that we can leave children's emotional and social development to parents... so schools have to provide the emotional and social guidance that some pupils currently lack. (DfES, 2003)

However, helping young people develop emotional resilience isn't just for young people from disturbed or disturbing backgrounds. School life and home life can be stressful for all young people, and with the growing awareness of the importance of emotional literacy, the *Promoting Children's Resilience and Wellbeing* series will be an ideal programme to support a key element, emotional resilience.

George Robinson and Barbara Maines

Developing Consideration, Respect and Tolerance is made up of teacher's notes, copiable stories and student activity sheets.

The teacher's notes:

▸ outline the programme, its rationale and relationship to curriculum outcomes

▸ provide ideas about introducing each topic via the relevant story, class and individual activities, discussion, role-play and extension exercises.

The values and story titles introduced in the programme are:

	Value	**Title**
1.	Consideration	Dream Manners
2.	Friendliness	Pasta Parcel
3.	Honesty	It Wasn't Me
4.	Kindness	The New Neighbours
5.	Responsibility	Poor Blackie
6.	Tolerance	My Aunt Mattie
7.	Confidence	Close Call
8.	Respect	Golden Triangle
9.	Courage	Jeff's Medal
10.	Determination	Lia's Leap
11.	Caring	Hop, Skip and Jump!
12.	Assertiveness	Just For Once

Schools are a major area for social interaction, making them vital environments for primary prevention programmes based on the framework of reducing risk and promoting protective factors in the lives of students. Primary prevention is about building belonging, and promoting the wellbeing of all students.

This programme is designed to assist students to understand the core prosocial values that support the development of a safe and positive learning environment, social connectedness and wellbeing.

Listed below are five protective factors that assist in promoting resilience and wellbeing in young people (Hawkins and Catalano et al., 1996).

1. To assist students to feel a sense of belonging and fitting in at school.

2. To identify a special talent or interest for which he/she is recognised and encouraged.

3. To promote proactive problem-solving.

4. To enhance a positive social orientation.

5. To encourage an optimistic sense of future.

Each of the Value topics within the programme are mapped against some of the identified protective factors.

Protective Factors Enhancing Resilience

VALUE AND STORY TITLE	Sense of belonging and fitting in.	Recognition of a special talent or gift.	Promoting proactive problem-solving.	Enhance positive social orientation.	Encourage an optimistic sense of future.
CONSIDERATION Dream Manners	✔		✔	✔	
FRIENDLINESS Pasta Parcel	✔	✔	✔	✔	✔
HONESTY It Wasn't Me	✔	✔		✔	
KINDNESS The New Neighbours	✔		✔	✔	✔
RESPONSIBILITY Poor Blackie	✔		✔		✔
TOLERANCE My Aunt Mattie	✔		✔		✔
CONFIDENCE Close Call		✔	✔		✔
RESPECT Golden Triangle	✔		✔	✔	✔
COURAGE Jeff's Medal	✔		✔	✔	✔
DETERMINATION Lia's Leap	✔		✔	✔	✔
CARING Hop, Skip and Jump	✔	✔	✔	✔	✔
ASSERTIVENESS Just For Once	✔	✔	✔	✔	✔

The programme may be used:

- ▸ to assist in the implementation of prosocial values and associated behaviours that help promote a safe and supportive whole-school environment, conducive to learning

- ▸ to assist in the identification and development of a 'language' of values and associated behaviours that promote student connectedness and engagement

- ▸ to assist in the identification and development of social competence (bridging and bonding) and communication skills

- ▸ to assist in the building of positive relationships with others, thus promoting emotional and social wellbeing

- ▸ to assist in the promotion of protective factors that enhance resilience

- ▸ to assist in the development, recognition and reinforcement of positive regard

- ▸ to assist in the implementation of the school's Health and Wellbeing programmes, working in the areas of both prevention and early intervention

- ▸ as a resource that promotes discussion and group work

- ▸ to assist in the promotion and development of strong school and parent/home links.

The topics may be dealt with sequentially or as individual units of work, depending on the teacher's and students' needs.

The stories within each unit have been designed to be read by the class teacher or facilitator. Alternatively, multiple copies of a story can be used for group reading.

The individual stories take approximately ten minutes to read. The time taken to complete each unit will also vary according to the depth in which each topic is examined, the activities undertaken and the level of student participation.

Story Values and Outcomes

Title: Dream Manners

Main Focus Value of Story: Consideration

Related Values to the Story

- Responsibility
- Courtesy
- Determination

Health and Wellbeing Outcomes

- Identifying behaviours that enhance personal relationships.
- Deciding right from wrong behaviour.
- Identifying major influences on behaviour towards others.
- Examining the impact of your actions on others.

Title: Pasta Parcel

Main Focus Value of Story: Friendliness

Related Values to the Story

- Helpfulness
- Cooperation
- Creativity
- Tolerance

Health and Wellbeing Outcomes

- Identifying individual talents and qualities.
- Identifying behaviours that affect relationships.
- Identifying behaviours that enhance relationships.

Title: It Wasn't Me

Main Focus Value of Story: Honesty

Related Values to the Story

- Responsibility
- Assertiveness
- Tolerance
- Trustworthiness

Health and Wellbeing Outcomes

- Deciding right from wrong behaviour.
- Identifying strategies to resolve conflict.
- Describing behaviours that affect relationships.

Title: The New Neighbours

Main Focus Value of Story: Kindness

Related Values to the Story

- Friendliness
- Caring
- Tolerance
- Helpfulness

Health and Wellbeing Outcomes

- Identifying characteristics and behaviours that enhance relationships.
- Examining the need to belong to a group.

Title: Poor Blackie

Main Focus Value of Story: Responsibility

Related Values to the Story

- Dependability
- Reliability
- Caring
- Communication

Health and Wellbeing Outcomes

- Identifying behaviours that can affect relationships.
- Identifying strategies to resolve conflicts.

Title: My Aunt Mattie

Main Focus Value of Story: Tolerance

Related Values to the Story

- Respect
- Responsibility
- Forgiveness

Health and Wellbeing Outcomes

- Describing how mutual trust, respect and tolerance are developed and demonstrated in relationships.
- Identifying behaviours that can enhance close relationships.

Title: Close Call

Main Focus Value of Story: Confidence

Related Values to the Story

- Caring
- Courage
- Consideration

Health and Wellbeing Outcomes

- Identifying feelings of safety and security.
- Encouraging a sense of belonging.

Title: Golden Triangle

Main Focus Value of Story: Respect

Related Values to the Story

- Responsibility
- Enthusiasm
- Honesty
- Tolerance
- Forgiveness

Health and Wellbeing Outcomes

- Identifying differing friendship expectations, roles and responsibilities, and how these affect relationships.

Title: Jeff's Medal

Main Focus Value of Story: Courage

Related Values to the Story

- Determination
- Kindness
- Caring
- Confidence

Health and Wellbeing Outcomes

- Identifying major influences that may affect a person's self-concept.
- Examining the importance of setting goals to achieve an outcome.
- Examining how meeting personal challenges can enhance feelings of self-worth.

Title: Lia's Leap

Main Focus Value of Story: Determination

Related Values to the Story

- Courage
- Creativity
- Determination

Health and Wellbeing Outcomes

- Explaining how meeting challenges and achieving goals can promote good feelings.

Title: Hop, Skip and Jump!

Main Focus Value of Story: Caring

Related Values to the Story

- Kindness
- Friendliness
- Consideration

Health and Wellbeing Outcomes

- Identifying feelings of safety and security.
- Encouraging a sense of belonging.
- Identifying individual talents and qualities.
- Identifying actions that may encourage self-worth in others.

Title: Just For Once

Main Focus Value of Story: Assertiveness

Related Values to the Story

- Confidence
- Determination
- Courage

Health and Wellbeing Outcomes

- Identifying strategies to resolve conflict.
- Examining behaviours that affect relationships.
- Describing how meeting challenges can increase feelings of self-worth.

Structure of the Programme

Each section introduces a Focus Value and has the following format:

▸ **Focus Value**

▸ **Objectives**

▸ **Factors Enhancing Resilience**

▸ **Introduction to the Focus Value** – definition brainstormed by students; discussion on how the value and related behaviours could be positively demonstrated in school.

▸ **The Story** – read by the class teacher or copied for individual students; class discussion and related questions.

▸ **Activities** – three to five copiable activity sheets related to the value. These may involve:

1. small group tasks

2. role-play scenarios

3. individual student application to a task

4. partner work.

Focus Values

Objectives

▸ To assist students to identify family expectations and understand that these may differ between families.

▸ To encourage students to examine roles and responsibilities, and learn how they may affect relationships.

Factors Enhancing Resilience

▸ Promoting a sense of belonging and fitting in.

▸ Promoting proactive problem-solving.

▸ Enhancing a positive social orientation.

Introduction to the Focus Value

As a class, or in small groups, brainstorm a definition of the focus value, 'consideration'. The students may wish to refer to a dictionary or thesaurus.

Ask the students to discuss how consideration can be shown at school. Ask them to list some of the behaviours that support the value of consideration.

The Story: Dream Manners

The story may be read to the students by the class teacher, or in small groups if multiple copies have been made.

Follow the story with a class discussion. Some suggested questions are:

▸ Why had Mary rushed to finish her geography page?

▸ What did the teacher say when she saw Mary's geography page?

▸ What was Mary told to do after she rushed to be first to finish her dinner?

▸ Why do we use words and expressions like please, thank you, excuse me and pardon me?

▸ Why did Dad send Mary off to find her manners?

▸ How could using manners support the value of consideration?

Materials

▸ Being Considerate activity sheet.

▸ Cartoon Time activity sheet.

▸ Acrostic Poem activity sheet.

▸ Consideration Poster.

▸ Coloured pen.

Dream Manners

Written by Helen Miles
Illustrated by Katie Jardine

Chapter 1

'I'm finished first!' Mary screamed out in class, making everyone jump. But when her teacher saw Mary's geography page, she said it was a dreadful jumble. Mary had to repeat it, and was the last to finish.

'I'm on that first!' Mary squealed, but the bell rang just as she sat on the swing.

'I'm out first!' cried Mary. But Mary's dress caught on the gate and she was last to leave school.

'I'm reading that first!' she screeched at her brother after school. But the old book fell to pieces as she snatched it, and she was unable to read it.

'I'm done first!' she yelled at the dinner table that night. But she pulled the tablecloth off when she leapt up to go. Mary was told to clean up the mess, and was the last one to leave the dining room.

'I'm going to be the first asleep too,' Mary said, scrunching up her eyes. But she thrashed around in bed unable to sleep.

'I'm up first, Dad. Let's do the gardening before the sun gets up!' she said on Saturday, jumping on to his bed. But she slipped off, taking the duvet with her. Mary's angry mother told her to go back to bed.

'See, I beat the sun!' Mary mumbled to herself while gulping down her breakfast. But Mary coughed and spluttered when her cereal went down the wrong way.

'I'll get the flashlight so I can be the first one to see,' Mary thought, stumbling down the back steps.

Not long after the sun peeped over the neighbourhood, Mary finished the planting. But later, when her father peered at the crooked row of seedlings, he was furious.

'I'll water them first,' Mary shrieked, turning on the hose and squirting her father.

'Show some consideration!' he roared. 'Go inside, young lady. And don't come out until you find your manners!'

Chapter 2

'Silly Dad,' Mary muttered, climbing the stairs. 'Manners can't be found.' But Mary decided she would pretend to look for them, just to please her father.

She looked under her bed, but they couldn't be there; it was packed with dusty old picture books and shoes.

She crashed back her wardrobe door and a mountain of clothes fell out. Her manners couldn't possibly fit in there.

She squinted into her teddy bear's ear, but they weren't in there either. It was full of fluff.

She opened her schoolbag, but closed it in a hurry. Her manners wouldn't stay in there with that mouldy cheese sandwich!

She lifted her toy box lid. No, her manners wouldn't be in there with all that broken junk.

She thumped downstairs and stretched open Muffin's mouth. The cat meowed loudly and ran away. Her manners were definitely not in there!

Mary rushed back upstairs. 'I know!' she giggled. 'They've gone to sleep.' She rummaged around under the covers, but her manners weren't there either.

'While I'm here, I'll be the first to have a nap,' Mary said, yawning. All the pretending had made her tired.

Mary drifted off to sleep and began to dream. She saw wiggly words popping up from the ground like flowers.

Soon, Mary awoke and bounded downstairs.

'I found my manners, Dad, like... considering others!' she said. 'They were growing in a garden in my dream.'

'Good,' he said. 'Now if you can really make them grow, I can be the FIRST to enjoy them!'

Being Considerate

Why do we use words and expressions like please, thank you, excuse me and pardon me?

_____

_____

_____

_____

_____

How does it make you feel when other people say thank you to you when you've done something for them?

_____

_____

_____

_____

_____

Cartoon Time

In the cartoon spaces below, draw a cartoon depicting a character being considerate, and a character who is not being considerate.

Cartoon: Being Considerate

1	2
3	4

Cartoon: Not Being Considerate

1	2
3	4

Acrostic Poem

Create an acrostic poem for the word consideration.

Include why, what, where, when and how consideration may be shown.

C _____

O _____

N _____

S _____

I _____

D _____

E _____

R _____

A _____

T _____

I _____

O _____

N _____

Consideration Poster

Being considerate to others helps our classrooms to be happy places. In the space below, design a poster that clearly illustrates how to show consideration at school.

Objectives

▶ To help students identify the various forms that friendship can take.

▶ To help students identify values and behaviours that promote a sense of belonging.

Factors Enhancing Resilience

▶ Promoting proactive problem-solving.

▶ Enhancing positive social orientation.

▶ Encouraging an optimistic sense of the future.

▶ Recognising a special talent.

▶ Promoting a sense of belonging and fitting in.

Introduction to the Focus Value

As a class, or in small groups, brainstorm a definition of the focus value, 'friendliness'. The students may wish to refer to a dictionary or thesaurus.

Ask the students to discuss how friendliness can be shown at school. Ask them to list some of the behaviours that support the value of friendliness.

The Story: Pasta Parcel

The story may be read to the students by the class teacher, or in small groups if multiple copies have been made.

Follow the story with a class discussion. Some suggested questions are:

▶ Why had Jairo chosen pasta for the food project?

▶ Why was Jairo feeling frustrated with Miklos?

▶ How did Miklos behave at school?

▶ How did Jairo and Miklos use each of their talents for their presentation?

▶ What do you think Miklos learnt about working with others and valuing different ideas and talents?

▶ Did the boys achieve their purpose?

▶ Sometimes friendship requires patience and understanding. In what ways was this demonstrated in the story?

Materials

▶ Friendship Qualities activity sheet.

▶ Togetherness activity sheet.

▶ Welcome activity sheet.

▶ Friendly Behaviours activity sheet.

Pasta Parcel

Written by Claire Saxby
Illustrated by Ian Moule

Chapter 1

'Man, this is the most boring project ever!' said Miklos. 'Couldn't you have picked a more exciting food, Spag?'

Jairo's face went red.

'There's lots of different spag... pastas,' he mumbled. 'At least I've done something!'

Jairo slumped into his chair. This project on pasta was Jairo's way of laughing at his own nickname. All of a sudden, it didn't seem very funny.

'OK. How can we jazz it up a bit?' Miklos looked thoughtful. 'We could decorate you with curly spaghetti. Nah, no one would notice the difference!' Jairo sunk his head on the table. 'What about puppets made of pasta?' Miklos continued.

'We could put on a play. Cool! Those potato ones could be for heads... what are they called?'

Miklos was pointing at the poster Jairo had made. It had lots of shapes of pasta with their names next to them.

'Gnocchi,' mumbled Jairo, but Miklos wasn't listening.

'Or we could cook every type of pasta and have a restaurant lunch, take orders and stuff. Yeah, let's do that!'

Jairo groaned. 'Miklos, we have seven days!' He held seven fingers up in Miklos's face. 'Get it? Seven. Next Thursday. Five, if you only count school days. We can't do anything like that.'

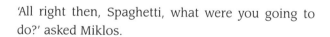

'All right then, Spaghetti, what were you going to do?' asked Miklos.

Jairo looked at his poster. 'I was just going to explain what all the different pastas are called and what they are used for.'

'Boring as...' Miklos rolled his eyes. 'OK, Miklos... you're so clever, you think of something!'

'I will!'

Chapter 2

'It's not fair!' Jairo kicked at a stain in the concrete.

'I do all the work, he does nothing, and now I have to share it all with him.' He sat down on the edge of a planter box, near where his grandmother was working.

'Do you want to ask the teacher if you can change partners?' Nanna asked as she dug the soil around the tomato bushes.

'No. The teacher asked me specially. He said I'd understand. But I don't.'

Jairo drew a face in the dirt. The face was frowning.

'He says things are difficult for Miklos at home. He says we all have to help him. But why is it only me that has to work with him? He's going to ruin my project.'

Nanna untied the rag holding the tomato bush to the stake.

'Do you think so?' She straightened the stake and re-tied the tomato to it. 'Is he really that bad?'

Jairo nodded. 'He makes everyone laugh when Mr Carlos is writing stuff on the board. Then we all get into trouble. He never reads the books we're all supposed to read. He never does his homework. Mr Carlos makes him sit out in the corridor sometimes, to do his work out there.' Jairo looked at Nanna. 'He's not even at school half the time. And he always calls me Jairo Spaghetti or Spaghetti Zanetti!'

Jairo made the frown on the face in the dirt bigger. Then he ran his fingers back and forward across the dirt, until there was no face left.

Nanna stood and brushed her hands on her apron. She glanced at his black curls, but said only, 'Let's get something to eat.'

Chapter 3

'We'll play the Pass the Parcel game,' said Miklos. 'We fill the parcel with sweets and I'll do the music and it'll be heaps of fun and...' Miklos was standing up, waving his arms about in the air.

'Hang on. What's that got to do with pasta?' This was a nightmare, thought Jairo.

'Pass the Parcel,' Miklos said. 'Get it? PAS-TA-Parcel!'

This was worse than a nightmare. At least you could wake up from a nightmare. Jairo pinched himself in case he was asleep. He wasn't.

'Miklos, it just won't work. It has to have something to do with the project. And in case you've forgotten, we have only three more days.'

Jairo was getting desperate. Miklos had promised he'd work something out over the weekend. Jairo knew he

shouldn't have trusted him. Now they were running out of time. Fast. 'This is hopeless. We'll never be ready in time,' Jairo sighed.

'I was only trying to help,' replied Miklos. His shoulders slumped as he looked up at the ceiling. 'I always get it wrong, don't I?' His voice was soft, so soft Jairo had to lean closer to hear him. 'It's easy for you. You always get it right. I wish I was good at stuff, good at everything, like you are.'

Jairo sat back in his chair. Miklos thought he was good at stuff. Wow. He never would have guessed. All Miklos ever seemed to do was make fun of Jairo. Jairo was silent for a minute.

'OK, Miklos, let's give Pasta Parcel a try.'

Chapter 4

Mr Carlos stood up. 'OK, class put your books away. It's time to present your projects. Who wants to go first?'

'We will,' called Miklos.

Mr Carlos glanced at Jairo. 'Are you ready?'

'Yes, Mr Carlos,' Jairo agreed. 'Can we use the tapeplayer, please?'

Mr Carlos lifted the tape player onto his desk.

'Our project is about all the different types of pasta.' Jairo paused. 'Can everyone sit in a circle on the floor?' He looked at Mr Carlos, who nodded.

When everyone was ready, Jairo looked at his partner.

'Ready, Miklos?'

'Ready.'

Jairo started the tape player and the music began. The children passed the parcel to each other, slowly at first and then faster, until Jairo stopped the tape.

'OK, Lia, take off the first layer,' said Jairo. 'Inside, you'll find a yellow piece of paper with the name of a type of pasta written on it.' Lia began unwrapping. 'Miklos will mime the common name and you have to guess it.'

'It says RAV... RAVIOLI,' said Lia. Miklos dropped to the floor and began snoring.

Everyone laughed. 'Is it sleepy pasta?' asked Lia.

Miklos pointed beneath his head.

'Bed pasta?'

'Hairy-head pasta?'

'Pillow pasta?'

Miklos jumped up and stretched.

'Yes,' said Jairo. 'It's pillow pasta. Sometimes it's filled with cheese, sometimes with meat.' He pointed to the chart he'd drawn then started the music again.

The class began passing the parcel. Jairo stopped it when it reached Roman.

'This one's MACARONI!' said Roman.

Jairo grinned. This was fun. Only Miklos could make miming elbow so funny. He was really good at performing.

Miklos mimed all the different pastas, but the best one was last.

Mr Carlos unwrapped the last layer of paper.

'It says FARFALLE,' said Mr Carlos, looking at Miklos.

Miklos pulled a colourful scarf around his shoulders. He began dancing across the room, flapping his arms, and the scarf, in the air.

'Scarf pasta?' guessed Mr Carlos. Everyone laughed again. Jairo shook his head.

'Ballerina!' said someone.

'Bird pasta!' said another.

'Butterfly!' guessed a third. Miklos stopped mid-flap.

'Got it!' said Jairo. 'Farfalle pasta is shaped like a butterfly or like a bow. It is often used in salads.' Miklos fluttered over to the board and pointed to the picture of farfalle.

'That's it,' said Jairo.

'The End,' agreed Miklos.

He walked over to Jairo and they bowed.

Everyone began clapping. Jairo and Miklos bowed again.

'Well done, boys!' Mr Carlos came over to Jairo. 'I knew I could rely on you, Jairo.'

Jairo looked at Miklos. 'I couldn't have done it by myself.'

'Yay, Spaghetti Zanetti!' echoed Miklos.

Friendship Qualities

Sometimes it's difficult to make friends because we can't see all the positive things we have to offer.

List ten good things about yourself that could be shared with a friend, for example, I have a great sense of humour.

My Friendship Qualities

1. _____

2. _____

3. _____

4. _____

5. _____

6. _____

7. _____

8. _____

9. _____

10. _____

Togetherness

Make a list of all the things you and your friends do together.

Draw you and your friends together.

My list

My illustration

Welcome

Answer the questions below.

How does your class make a new student feel welcome?

_____

_____

_____

What does your teacher do?

_____

_____

_____

What do you do?

_____

_____

_____

Create a poem about friendship based on the formula of:

Roses are red,

Violets are blue.

Friends stick together,

Like me and you.

Or use your own rhyme.

_____

_____

_____

_____

_____

_____

_____

Friendly Behaviours

In groups, create a checklist of friendly behaviours that help the class work well together. For example:

- ▶ use of manners
- ▶ being cooperative with others
- ▶ friendly gestures
- ▶ speaking pleasantly
- ▶ sharing class materials
- ▶ taking turns
- ▶ being patient.

Checklist

1. _____

2. _____

3. _____

4. _____

5. _____

6. _____

7. _____

8. _____

9. _____

10. _____

Create a short play that demonstrates some items from your group's checklist. Ask the audience to identify the elements of 'friendship promoting behaviours' from your checklist.

Objectives

▶ To help students identify major values they consider when deciding right from wrong behaviour.

▶ To encourage students to examine roles and responsibilities, and learn how these may affect relationships.

Factors Enhancing Resilience

▶ Promoting a sense of fitting in or belonging.

▶ Recognising a special talent or gift.

▶ Promoting proactive problem-solving.

▶ Enhancing positive social orientation.

▶ Encouraging an optimistic sense of future.

Introduction to the Focus Value

As a class, or in small groups, brainstorm a definition of the focus value, 'honesty'. The students may wish to refer to a dictionary or thesaurus.

Ask the students to discuss how honesty can be shown at school. Ask them to list some of the behaviours that support the value of honesty.

The Story: It Wasn't Me!

The story may be read to the students by the class teacher, or in small groups if multiple copies have been made.

Follow the story with a class discussion. Some suggested questions are:

▶ What did Ms Foster think Michael and Laura had done?

▶ Why did Laura lie? What did she say?

▶ How did Laura feel about Michael lying about her?

▶ Why did Laura tell Tiffany a lie about Michael?

▶ What advice did Laura's mum give her? Do you think it was good advice?

▶ What did Michael say it felt like when Laura lied about him?

Materials

▶ Telling Lies activity sheet.

▶ Honesty is the Best policy activity sheet.

▶ Being Honest activity sheet

▶ Discussion – Wisdom in a Fable activity sheet.

▶ Coloured pens.

It Wasn't Me

Written by Leanne Winfield
Illustrated by Luke McFarlane

Chapter 1

Laura and Michael sat outside Ms Foster's room. They were in big trouble. Someone had taken a soccer ball without permission and it had been kicked over the fence. It had then been run over by a car, squashed flat and ruined.

The headteacher, Ms Foster, had seen Laura and Michael near the fence. They had been told to come inside and wait.

'Don't tell her! OK, Laura?'

'I don't want to lie about it, Michael,' she told him. 'How did Vince get away? Why is he the one who never gets caught?'

Just then, Ms Foster came out of her room. 'I'll see you first, Michael,' she said.

Nervously, Laura tapped her feet against the bottom of the chair. It wasn't very long before Michael came back out. She tried to catch his eye, but he had his head down and he didn't look at her.

'You can come in now, Laura,' Ms Foster said. 'So, Laura, what happened?'

'I don't know, Ms Foster,' she lied.

'Did you see the soccer ball that was taken from the sports store?'

'Yes. I saw someone kick it, but I don't know who it was.'

'Was it Michael?'

'I don't know.'

'Michael said he saw you take the ball and kick it over the fence.'

'What? He couldn't have said that, because it's not true,' Laura said angrily.

'Well, he did say that. So unless I hear more from you than 'I don't know', I'll have to believe his story.'

Laura was silent. Was Ms Foster trying to trick her into telling? Surely Michael wouldn't have told a lie like that.

'Do you have anything else to say, Laura?'

'No, Ms Foster, I haven't.'

'I'll be speaking to your mother about this.'

'Yes, Ms Foster,' she replied, gritting her teeth to stop her mouth from exploding.

Chapter 2

'I'm sorry. I can explain,' Michael whispered as Laura walked past him into the classroom without even looking at him. 'I'll tell you after school.'

'What's the matter with you?' Tiffany asked as Laura sat at the desk beside her.

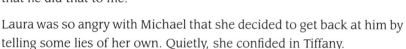

'It's Michael. He told a lie about me. Now I'm in big trouble. Ms Foster's going to ring my mum. I can't believe that he did that to me.'

Laura was so angry with Michael that she decided to get back at him by telling some lies of her own. Quietly, she confided in Tiffany.

'You know, I'm not surprised about Michael. After all, the other day I saw him steal his brother's bag of marbles. And last week, he took some money that his mum had left on the kitchen bench. We'll have to be careful, he might start taking things here, too.'

Chapter 3

At home that night, Mum told Laura that Ms Foster had phoned about the soccer ball.

'It wasn't me, Mum. Michael lied about me.'

'What did he say?'

'He told Ms Foster that I had taken the soccer ball from the storeroom and kicked it onto the road.'

'And did you?'

'No.'

'Did he do it?'

'No.'

'Who did it then?'

'Michael's friend, Vince.'

'Why didn't you tell Ms Foster it was Vince?'

'Michael asked me not to. But I didn't think that he'd put the blame onto me. Anyway, I got him back. I told a couple of lies to Tiffany about him. Tomorrow, they will be all over the school.'

'That's not a good thing to do, Laura. He didn't treat you fairly, but you've done the same thing to him. Two wrongs don't make a right, as the old saying goes.'

'I was angry with him.'

'It would have been more honest if you'd told him that.'

Laura thought about what her mother had said to her, and then decided what to do.

Later that evening, Laura told her mother that she would tell Ms Foster the truth.

'I think you, Michael and Vince should tell Ms Foster the truth together. Why don't you phone them now?' suggested her mother.

'Great idea,' said Laura.

Chapter 4

The next day, Michael and Vince found Laura with some friends before school started.

Tiffany called out to Michael, 'We're watching you, sticky fingers!'

'Actually, he doesn't steal,' Laura said. 'I was angry with Michael yesterday, so I lied about him. Sorry.'

'It's awful when someone tells lies about you,' Michael said. 'I know that now. Sorry, Laura. After you rang me last night, I rang Vince and we decided to tell the truth. We know we're going to get into trouble, but we want to stop worrying and arguing about it.'

'Ready to see Ms Foster, then?' Laura asked Michael and Vince.

'Yes,' they answered together.

Chapter 5

'Ms Foster, I lied yesterday when I said Laura took the ball and kicked it over the fence. It was Vince,' Michael admitted.

'And I lied about not knowing who took the ball and who kicked it over the fence. I knew that it was Vince,' Laura confessed.

'After I took the ball and accidentally kicked it over the fence, I ran to the playground,' Vince said. 'I left Laura and Michael to take the blame.'

'Why didn't you own up?' Ms Foster asked Vince.

'I want to go away with Michael and his uncle on the weekend. If I've been in trouble, my parents won't let me go.'

'Me too,' Michael said. 'Sorry for lying about you, Laura. I just couldn't say that it was Vince.'

'Well, you have now,' Ms Foster said. 'I'm pleased that you've all finally told the truth. But you should own up to things right away. You always get into more trouble if you try to get out of it, especially if you lie.'

'We know that now, Ms Foster,' Michael said.

'I'll be phoning your parents to discuss a suitable punishment. Perhaps you could also do some fundraising for new soccer balls for the school. For the moment, you can pick up any rubbish that is in the playground.'

'I'm not going to lie about anyone, or for anyone again,' Laura declared.

'Neither am I,' said Michael.

'I've learnt my lesson, too,' added Vince. 'Next time, I'm not taking a ball without permission and I'm not going to lie about anything anymore!'

Telling Lies

Answer the questions below.

Should you lie if a friend asks you to? Explain your answer.

_____

_____

_____

_____

_____

What usually happens to friendships when people lie to each other?

_____

_____

_____

_____

_____

If a person tells a lie, what usually happens?

_____

_____

_____

_____

_____

Why is it usually better to be honest about things when they happen?

_____

_____

_____

_____

_____

Honesty is the Best Policy

What do you think is meant by the saying, 'Honesty is the best policy'?

_____

_____

_____

_____

_____

_____

_____

In the box below, design a sign or poster with a slogan about being honest.

Being Honest

Some people gain a reputation for being honest, and some for being not quite so honest.

Below are some statements. Tick the statements that you think would probably be honest

I eat six truckloads of bananas a day. ☐

My uncle has been to Mars and is now on his way to Pluto. ☐

I go to school. ☐

My dog climbs trees and swings by his tail. ☐

I had a birthday last year. ☐

I can go seven days without any sleep. ☐

I will have lunch at school today. ☐

My teacher has horns on his/her head. ☐

One day this week, I will have sport. ☐

I have an elephant in my back garden. ☐

I can be honest. ☐

On the back of this sheet, list and draw three honest things about yourself.

Discussion – Wisdom in a Fable

Read the fable of The Boy Who Cried Wolf to the students.

Using the idea portrayed in this fable, discuss with students the need for honesty when relating to other people, as in the fable.

Ask the students to create a play that displays elements of the fable, or they may like to act out The Boy Who Cried Wolf in groups.

Discuss the possible effects on people when someone is continually dishonest with others. Ensure that students understand the importance of personal reputation as far as credibility in the community goes.

Objectives

▶ To help students identify the various forms that kindness can take.

▶ To help students identify values and behaviours that promote a sense of belonging and a sense of safety.

Factors Enhancing Resilience

▶ Promoting a sense of belonging or fitting in.

▶ Promoting proactive problem-solving.

▶ Enhancing a positive social orientation.

▶ Encouraging an optimistic sense of future.

Introduction to the Focus Value

As a class, or in small groups, brainstorm a definition of the focus value, 'kindness'. The students may wish to refer to a dictionary or thesaurus.

Ask the students to discuss how kindness can be shown at school. Ask them to list some of the behaviours that support the value of kindness.

The Story: The New Neighbours

The story may be read to the students by the class teacher, or in small groups if multiple copies have been made.

Follow the story with a class discussion. Some suggested questions are:

▶ Why were Beth and Steve excited when the new neighbours arrived?

▶ When Beth's family went to meet the new neighbours, what did they take and why?

▶ What did Beth's mum and dad offer to lend the new neighbours?

▶ On Promila's first day at school, how was Beth kind to her?

▶ Where did Promila say her family had come from?

▶ What did Deepa invite everyone to do the following weekend and why?

▶ What do you think it would be like to move to a new country? What would be the good things about the move? What problems do you think there might be?

Materials

▶ Kindness Award activity sheet.

▶ A Difficult Situation activity sheet.

▶ Being Kind activity sheet.

▶ What Kindness Means to Me activity sheet.

▶ Coloured pens.

▶ Large pieces of paper.

The New Neighbours

Written by Leanne Winfield
Illustrated by Katie Jardine

Chapter 1

On a rainy Saturday morning, Beth watched a van pull into the driveway next door.

'Mum! Dad!' she called. 'There are people moving in next door!'

Mum, Dad and Steve all ran to the window. A tall, dark-haired man and a woman wearing a white scarf around her head got out of the front seat of a car. Three children climbed out of the back.

'Hooray! Our new neighbours have children!' Beth and Steve cheered. 'When can we meet them, Mum?'

'Perhaps tomorrow. Let's give them some time to settle in.'

Chapter 2

The next day, Beth's family went next door. Beth had picked a bunch of daffodils from the garden, Steve had collected some apples from the apple tree and Mum had baked sultana scones. Dad knocked on the front door. It was answered by the woman in the scarf.

'Hi, I'm Nick from next door and this is my wife, Jennie,' Beth's dad began.

'Hello. This is our daughter, Beth, and our son, Steve,' Mum said. 'Welcome to the neighbourhood.' They handed the woman their gifts.

'Thank you,' she said with a smile. 'My name is Deepa. Please come in and meet my family.'

There was not much furniture in the house. Perhaps they have another van coming later, Beth thought. They followed the woman towards the smell of exotic spices coming from the kitchen.

The man sat at the table with a child. The other two children were washing the dishes at the sink. Two broken chairs sat next to the back door.

'This is my husband, Rahul, and our children Promila, Vinod and Nalin.' She introduced Beth and her family to her husband and showed him the gifts.

'Thank you,' Rahul said. 'We are very pleased to be here.'

'Just thought we'd stop by. If there's anything we can help you with, let us know,' Dad said, smiling.

'We could lend you a couple of chairs if you'd like,' Mum offered.

'That is very kind of you,' Rahul said, 'but...' Deepa coughed and caught Rahul's eye. 'Thank you. We will be glad to borrow your chairs for a little while,' Rahul replied.

'Happy to help. I'll leave them for you on your front doorstep. We'll see you again soon,' Dad said.

'It was nice to meet you,' Mum added as Deepa and Rahul walked Beth's family to the front door.

Chapter 3

The next morning, Beth and Steve set off for school. They wondered if Promila, Vinod and Nalin would start school that day.

There was the usual Monday morning assembly then the children went to their classrooms. Not long after that, Promila came into Beth's classroom.

Miss Hartley introduced Promila to the class and asked if someone would show Promila around the school.

'Miss Hartley, could I, please?' Beth asked her teacher.

'Certainly Beth,' Miss Hartley replied.

'Hi Promila,' Beth said with a friendly smile. 'I'm so glad you're in my class. Come and meet my friend. This is Katya.'

'Hello, Katya. It is good to meet you,' Promila said.

Chapter 4

For the rest of the day, Beth and Katya showed Promila around the school and helped her with her work. After school, Promila had to meet Vinod and Nalin at the front gate. They all walked home together.

'Where did you move from?' Beth asked Promila.

'From India,' she said.

'That must be far away.'

'Yes. It has been a long journey and we left with nothing. But now we have a home.'

'Is that why you don't have much furniture?'

'Yes. My uncle and aunt have given us some things.'

'Would you like to come to my place when we get home?' Beth asked.

'Yes, but I'll have to ask my mother first.'

Chapter 5

During the week, Beth and Katya spent a lot of time with Promila. Vinod went along with Steve and joined the local junior football team and attended training. Nalin practised kicking the football while he watched the training sessions.

On the weekend, Mum and Dad invited some of the neighbours over for lunch to meet Rahul, Deepa, Promila, Vinod and Nalin. Each family brought a dish to add to the table.

'We have made nan, some bread, a Tandoori Chicken, spicy but not very hot, and some rice,' Rahul said.

'It smells delicious,' Mum said, taking the plates from Rahul and Deepa. Eventually, everyone sat down to eat and chat. Rahul, a plumber, and Deepa, an accountant, were offered suggestions for starting work.

After lunch, Steve and Vinod organised the children into two teams and they played footy in the back garden. Vinod had learnt quickly at footy training. Nalin copied the others' actions.. Some of the grown-ups, including Rahul, joined in as well.

'I don't understand this game,' Rahul said, laughing. 'Perhaps we should play cricket instead.'

Beth overheard Deepa say to Jennie, 'Next weekend, you must all come to lunch at our house. We will set up a cricket pitch. But we will have to ask you to bring your own chairs!'

Kindness Award

In the space below, design an award that you might give someone for his/her kindness.

A Difficult Situation

Write about a time when you used kindness to help someone who was in a difficult situation.

_____

_____

_____

_____

_____

_____

_____

_____

_____

_____

_____

_____

Illustrate your achievement in the box below.

Being Kind

List six different things that you could do at school to show kindness among students.

1. _____

2. _____

3. _____

4. _____

5. _____

6. _____

In the space below, design a new toy that shows kindness.

On a large piece of paper, create a board game for two people, based on acts of kindness.

What Kindness Means to Me

Complete the Y chart below.

Draw what kindness looks like to you.

Draw the colour and shape that would represent kindness for you.

Write what kindness feels like for you.

_____

_____

_____

_____

_____

_____

_____

_____

_____

_____

_____

_____

Objectives

▸ To help students identify the various forms responsibility may take.

▸ To help students identify values and behaviours that assist in the process of social connectedness.

Factors Enhancing Resilience

▸ Promoting a sense of belonging and fitting in.

▸ Promoting proactive problem-solving.

▸ Encouraging an optimistic sense of future.

Introduction to the Focus Value

As a class, or in small groups, brainstorm a definition of the focus value, 'responsibility'. The students may wish to refer to a dictionary or thesaurus.

Ask the students to discuss how responsibility can be shown at school. Ask them to list some of the behaviours that support the value of responsibility.

The Story: Poor Blackie

The story may be read to the students by the class teacher, or in small groups if multiple copies have been made.

Follow the story with a class discussion. Some suggested questions are:

▸ How did Hari and Ankita earn their pocket money?

▸ Why did Hari think that Ankita should feed Blackie?

▸ Why didn't Ankita feed Blackie?

▸ Before Ankita left for school, what did she tell Blackie?

▸ What was the first thing Blackie did when Ankita arrived home from school?

▸ When did Hari think he and Ankita were swapping chores?

▸ Why did their mum say they had been irresponsible?

▸ Who had paid the price?

▸ Why is it important to be responsible and make sure you do your chores?

Materials

▸ Being Responsible activity sheet.

▸ Cartoon Time activity sheet.

▸ Acrostic Poem activity sheet.

▸ Responsibility at School activity sheet.

▸ Coloured pens.

Poor Blackie

Written by Leanne Winfield
Illustrated by Peta Taylor

Chapter 1

Mum and Dad gave us pocket money for helping around the house. Every day, my older brother, Hari, fed Blackie the dog and emptied the rubbish bin. I fed Bill the budgie and took the dishes from the table to the kitchen.

One day, we were both in the kitchen sorting out the pet food.

'Maybe we should swap, Ankita. It would make more sense if one person fed Blackie and Bill,' Hari said.

I was thinking that Hari probably wanted to feed the animals, but I didn't want to take out the rubbish. What a messy job that was sometimes.

'But Bill doesn't have to be fed every day. His water has to be refilled and the seed checked. Blackie has to be fed once a day. I'm not sure I want to swap.'

'You're much better with animals than I am, Ankita. Anyway, I know you don't want to take out the

rubbish,' Hari said. 'I'll take out the rubbish and clear the table.'

'All right,' I agreed. 'I'll feed Blackie and Bill.'

Chapter 2

The next morning, I fed Bill the budgie. Hari hadn't cleared the breakfast dishes from the table.

He must be thinking we'll swap over after we get this week's pocket money, I thought. So I took the dishes to the kitchen sink. As I went out of the side door, Blackie jumped up at me and barked.

Hari must be taking his time getting ready this morning, I thought.

'Hari will feed you soon, Blackie,' I said as I left to meet my friend to walk to school.

Chapter 3

When I arrived home from school, Blackie was sitting at the back door whining. He looked at me with big, sad eyes.

I threw the dried old tennis ball around the garden for a while until it was covered in slobber. Then I got out the brush and started to groom Blackie's coat. He wouldn't sit still. He kept going over to his bowl and licking it.

'You are such a hungry dog! People must think we never feed you. Hari will be home to give you your dinner soon,' I told him.

Chapter 4

When Hari came home, he saw me checking the water in Bill's cage. Mum was starting to cook our dinner.

'How's the pet feeding going, Ankita?' he asked.

'Budgie feeder, you mean. We're swapping at the start of next week.'

'I thought we were going to swap this morning.'

'But you didn't clear the dishes this morning,' I told him.

'I forgot,' he admitted.

'Did you feed Blackie this morning?' I asked.

'No. I thought you did.'

'But I thought you were going to do it, Hari!'

Chapter 5

'Poor Blackie,' Mum said. 'I wonder how one of you would feel if we forgot to feed you! Or argued about it. You have both been very irresponsible, and the poor dog has paid the price.'

Hari and I looked at each other. We looked back at Blackie sitting at the side door, banging his tail against the glass. If we had just checked with each other, Blackie would not have missed being fed.

'Poor Blackie!' we both said, reaching for the tin of food to fill his bowl.

'I promise to communicate better and not to forget to feed you again, Blackie,' I said.

'And I promise to do my jobs when I should and to feed you if Ankita doesn't,' said Hari.

Blackie gave us each a great big, slobbery lick on the face before tucking into his dinner.

Being Responsible

Answer the questions below.

When is it important to be responsible? Give examples.

_____

_____

_____

_____

_____

_____

Make a list of some different situations in which you are expected to be responsible, for example, at home, in school and with friends.

_____

_____

_____

_____

_____

_____

_____

Make a list of different people in the community (for example, doctors, dentists and the police) who you expect to behave responsibly, and why it's important that they do so.

_____

_____

_____

_____

_____

_____

Cartoon Time

In the spaces below, draw a cartoon, using yourself as a character, about a time when you were responsible.

Acrostic Poem

With a partner, create an acrostic poem for the word 'responsibility'.

R _____

E _____

S _____

P _____

O _____

N _____

S _____

I _____

B _____

I _____

L _____

I _____

T _____

Y _____

Responsibility at School

Being responsible helps our classrooms to be happy places. In the space below, design a poster that clearly displays what you need to be responsible for at school.

Objectives

▸ To help students identify how being tolerant of others can enhance relationships.

▸ To help students understand that sometimes we need to practise tolerance to solve problems and challenges.

▸ To help students identify the value of tolerance in the development of a positive social orientation.

Factors Enhancing Resilience

▸ Promoting a sense of belonging and fitting in.

▸ Promoting proactive problem-solving.

▸ Enhancing a positive social orientation.

▸ Encouraging an optimistic sense of future.

Introduction to the Focus Value

As a class, or in small groups, brainstorm a definition of the focus value, 'tolerance'. The students may wish to refer to a dictionary or thesaurus.

Ask the students to discuss how tolerance can be shown at school. Ask them to list some of the behaviours that support the value of tolerance.

The Story: My Aunt Mattie

The story may be read to the students by the class teacher, or in small groups if multiple copies have been made.

Follow the story with a class discussion. Some suggested questions are:

▸ Why did Grandma think it was a good idea for Aunt Mattie to stay with Dad and David?

▸ When Aunt Mattie arrived, what did David notice about her appearance?

▸ Aunt Mattie showed her photos. Where had she been?

▸ How did David describe Aunt Mattie to Ben? How was she different from David's mum?

▸ What did Aunt Mattie do that David thought she was too old to do?

▸ What did Aunt Mattie say about David's crocodile socks?

▸ Why did David decide that Aunt Mattie might fit in pretty well after all?

▸ What advice would you give a friend who had someone new coming to live with them? For example, a step-parent, a new brother or sister or a grandparent.

Materials

▸ Being Tolerant activity sheet.

▸ Practicing Tolerance activity sheet.

▸ Tolerant Friend activity sheet.

▸ Appreciating Others activity sheet.

▸ Coloured pens.

My Aunt Mattie

Written by Helen Miles
Illustrated by Katie Jardine

Chapter 1

My Aunt Mattie arrives today, and it's all Grandma's fault!

'David is growing up,' she would say over and over. 'It's time you two had a woman around the house again.' And last week, Dad finally gave in.

But if we can't have Mum back, I don't want anyone. Dad and I are used to being on our own now, and we like it.

We eat hamburgers without plates, Digger is allowed to sleep on my bed, and I wear my favourite socks two days in a row. And we do the dishes when we feel like it, except when Grandma is coming to visit.

Aunt Mattie is Mum's sister, but I can't remember her. Dad says she's an old hippie, and that she's travelled everywhere. Well, I wish she would just keep on travelling.

Chapter 2

Aunt Mattie arrives not long after we finish giving Digger a bath.

I look at her jangling beads and her black floppy dress. And her hair! It's bright tomato-red and sticks up everywhere... nothing like Mum's neat hairstyle.

Digger barks and jumps all over her.

'Say hi to Aunt Mattie, Davo,' Dad says.

I mumble, 'Hello.'

'At least she doesn't fuss over me like Grandma,' I think, as I drag Digger outside to play.

'This is when I was in Africa,' Aunt Mattie tells Dad later, as she points to a photo. 'That lion followed our jeep for ages.'

'Come and have a look, Davo.'

I take a peek. Wow, that lion is big! But anyone can see lions at the zoo.

'I'm going to Ben's place,' I say.

Chapter 3

'Did your aunt arrive?' Ben asks.

'Yep.'

'What's she like?'

'She's weird. Not a bit like my mum. But at least she didn't kiss me.'

'You're lucky. My aunts slobber all over me!'

'She's been to Africa… and seen lions.'

'Cool!'

'Yeah,' I say. 'But her living with us isn't cool!'

When I arrive home, Aunt Mattie's books and photos are all over the coffee table. Boy, is she messy! Not a bit like my mum.

Then I walk to the kitchen. It looks like a hurricane has hit it. Dishes, pots and pans, and bits of food all over the place! And what's that funny smell? I peer around and see smoke wafting from a little stick. Aunt Mattie is burning that incense stuff. Mum used to burn it sometimes. I'd hated it, but at least Mum's hadn't smelt like Digger's poo!

Grabbing a drink, I go upstairs to finish my wild animal assignment. As I search through magazines for more pictures, I hear screams from the back garden.

I look out the window. Aunt Mattie, Digger and Dad are having a water fight. Dad and Digger, both dripping wet, are running away from Aunt Mattie, who chases them with the hose. Sort of looks like fun. But isn't she a bit old to be having water fights?

Mum would never have done that!

'Davo!' Dad yells. 'Aunt Mattie's cooked dinner. Come and get it!'

Oh great! I think. Probably slimy seaweed and yucky pumpkin seeds. Mum used to eat that sort of disgusting food sometimes, but she never made us eat it.

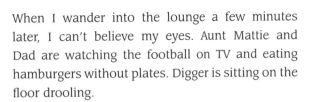

When I wander into the lounge a few minutes later, I can't believe my eyes. Aunt Mattie and Dad are watching the football on TV and eating hamburgers without plates. Digger is sitting on the floor drooling.

I squirm in between Dad and Aunt Mattie, slip off my boots, put my feet up on the coffee table and wiggle my crocodile socks.

'Groovy socks, David,' Aunt Mattie says. She doesn't say a word about them being dirty or my big toe sticking out.

Chapter 4

On Saturdays, my Aunt Mattie likes to come to the football with us. When our side scores a goal, Aunt Mattie cheers along. I sneak a look at her, and she looks down and winks, just like Mum used to.

And even though she will never replace my mum, I have decided that she might fit in pretty well after all.

I giggle when I think of the look on Grandma's face when she sees this place.

I reach for the photo album and wonder if Aunt Mattie has any spare photos for my assignment.

Being Tolerant

Sometimes, with our friends, we need to be tolerant. We need to be able to give and take on some things so that we may all get along. On the chart below, list the ways you demonstrate tolerance in friendship activities and classroom routines, for example, I am willing to play with different students sometimes.

Identify Activity For example, at sport	Demonstration of Tolerance I make sure everyone has a turn
1.	
2.	
3.	
4.	
5.	
6.	
7.	
8.	
9.	
10.	

Practising Tolerance

Often, we need to be more tolerant in the way we think people should look or behave. In the story *My Aunt Mattie*, David makes this discovery. List below the observations and comparisons David makes between his mother and aunt.

David's Mother	Aunt Mattie

Describe how David practised tolerance, and how you think it may impact on his relationship with his aunt.

_____

_____

_____

_____

_____

_____

_____

Tolerant Friend

Create a new toy for young children called the Tolerant Friend.

Illustrate and label the moving parts.

Design an eye-catching advertisement or packaging for your new toy.

Appreciating Others

A great way to help us understand and practise tolerance is through 'appreciation'.

In groups discuss these questions:

‣ What does appreciation mean?

‣ How does appreciation impact on your level of tolerance towards someone?

Using the story *My Aunt Mattie,* list some of the things that David appreciated about his aunt. (This may help you to feel more tolerant with others.)

1. _____

2. _____

3. _____

4. _____

5. _____

6. _____

List two qualities that you appreciate about each individual member of your family.

Member of family	Qualities
	1. 2.
	1. 2.
	1. 2.
	1. 2.

Objectives

▸ To help students identify the various forms that confidence can take.

▸ To help students identify behaviours and values that promote a sense of belonging and a sense of safety.

Factors Enhancing Resilience

▸ Recognition of a special talent or gift.

▸ Promoting proactive problem-solving.

▸ Encouraging an optimistic sense of future.

Introduction to the Focus Value

As a class, or in small groups, brainstorm a definition of the focus value, 'confidence'. The students may wish to refer to a dictionary or thesaurus.

Ask the students to discuss how confidence can be shown at school. Ask them to list some of the behaviours that support the value of confidence.

The Story: Close Call

The story may be read to the students by the class teacher, or in small groups if multiple copies have been made.

Follow the story with a class discussion. Some suggested questions are:

▸ What is confidence?

▸ How was confidence and lack of confidence portrayed in the story?

▸ What type of behaviours could be classified as confident behaviours?

▸ Why do people like feeling confident?

Materials

▸ Showing Confidence activity sheet.

▸ Survey activity sheet.

▸ Survey Results activity sheet.

▸ I Feel Confident activity sheet.

▸ Signals and Strategies activity sheet.

▸ Card and laminating material.

▸ Coloured pens.

▸ Newpapers and magazines.

Close Call

Written by Helen Miles
Illustrated by Ian Moule

Chapter 1

The chilly night wind rustled leaves on the forest floor. Pete looked up at the skinny moon grinning sideways at him through the massive pine trees, and shuddered.

Something scurried past him in the dark. He jumped with fright.

Suddenly, there was another noise, this time, a low rumbling growl. Peter froze. Trembling, he gulped a deep breath and took a hesitant step forward. He listened for another growl, but the forest was quiet now, just the wind whistling through the trees and the bugs scratching around in his bug catcher.

He relaxed a little and moved on, hoping he was heading the right way. Their campsite was near a stream and a large outcrop of rocks. He knew that, but in which direction?

It seemed like hours since he'd set out on a bug collecting expedition. The discovery of all sorts of new creepy-crawlies had fascinated him, and he hadn't noticed darkness creeping over the forest. Now he was lost, cold and frightened.

With shaking hands, he clutched his bug catcher. Dad will be looking for me by now, he thought. Maybe I should make some noise, just in case he's close.

'Row, row, row your boat gently down the stream…' he sang.

Pete walked on singing, his eyes straining and his body tense. I might be going further away from the campsite. Maybe I should stay in one place, he thought. Stopping once again, he looked up at the moon and wished the murky light would somehow filter down and light up the forest floor.

He would feel so much better if he could see more clearly. But he knew this wasn't going to happen. The only things that he could see clearly were the giant treetops swaying in the icy currents of air. And that was the way it would stay until morning.

Chapter 2

Pete rubbed his arms. The gloom seemed to be pressing in on him from all sides, and the damp was creeping into his bones. He moved and leant against a tree, hoping for some warmth.

Then his skin crawled. An overwhelming feeling that he was being watched swept through him. Swinging around, his eyes wide, he scanned the dim forest.

Then something touched his hand!

'Aaarggh!' Pete dropped his bug catcher and bolted, running blindly in the dark. He stumbled over a fallen branch and sprawled onto the ground. Without getting up, he peered over his shoulder.

What was it? Where was it? He cringed, covering his head with his arms, expecting to be attacked at any second. His ears strained to pick up any noise, but all he could hear now was his own raspy breathing.

Just as Pete peeped through his arms, a dim, shadowy shape moved stealthily toward him. His body erupted in a mass of goose bumps. He slid further away. With eyes like saucers, he stared as the shape seemed to come closer, then it hesitated.

Pete backed up against a tree. Maybe it can't see me now, he thought, his heart thumping. He twitched as an owl hooted somewhere above. Then he heard another noise, a whispering moan.

Terrified, he stared into the blackness. Damp pine needles stuck through his shorts and he felt a tingling in his nose.

'Oh no, I'm going to sneeze… a-a-aarrchoo!'

The forest came alive. Unseen things darted and flapped and cried out around him. The shadowy shape was on the move again, heading straight for him.

He heard another whimpering noise, much closer this time. Running probably isn't going to work, he thought. Whatever it is will eventually track me down and…

Pete braced himself for whatever was to follow.

In a heartbeat, the shape loomed over him. He was engulfed in total blackness.

Chapter 3

'Are you lost too?' the shape asked.

'Aahhhh!' Pete's cry died in his throat. 'What? Who?' he stuttered, limp with relief. It was human, not some ferocious creature.

'You nearly scared me to death!' Pete yelled, blinking at the little girl standing above him. 'Why didn't you say something sooner?'

'I did, but you were too busy singing and running and screaming. And I was scared too!' She sat beside him and hugged her knees up to her chest. 'Do you know the way out?' she asked, straightening her hat. 'My mum will be really worried.'

'No,' Pete answered shakily. He looked closely at her. She's younger than I am, probably about seven or eight, he thought.

'How come you're lost?' he asked.

'I was picking wildflowers. Then it got dark and I couldn't find my way back.'

'Everyone will be searching. They'll find us soon,' Pete said, sounding surer than he felt. 'What's your name?'

'Amelia,' she answered, as a huge shiver ran through her small body. 'I'm so-o-o cold.'

Pete realised they must get warm or they'd both freeze to death before anyone could find them. Amelia started to cry.

'Don't do that,' Pete said, frowning. 'Let's try to figure out how to get warm.'

Sniffing, Amelia wiped her tears with her sleeve. 'We could build a fire.'

'No matches, and anyway, it's too dark to find wood. I think we should find some cover.'

Holding hands, they crept forward, both searching the dimness for some sort of protection.

'This might be OK,' suggested Pete, peering inside a huge, dead tree trunk.

'What about spiders?' Amelia asked, her teeth chattering. 'I hate spiders.'

Pete sighed, but didn't say anything. He went in first and stomped around. 'That should have scared them all away. Now, come in before you turn into an icicle.'

Amelia nodded and scrambled in. She huddled up beside Pete, trying to control her shivering.

'They mightn't see us in here,' she said a few minutes later.

'You're right. Give me your hat.' Pete reached outside and stabbed Amelia's hat on a broken branch.

They covered themselves with dried bark and leaves, and waited. Three yawns later, Amelia was asleep, her head on Pete's shoulder. Not long after, he was asleep too.

Chapter 4

Some time during the night, Pete stirred. He thought he heard leaves crunching and footsteps close by. But he dropped off to sleep again almost immediately, and dreamed of a vaguely familiar voice calling his name.

Something slithered over Pete's foot. He twitched and shook his leg, his eyes shooting open. A small lizard darted away as Pete blinked at the bright sunshine beaming through the gaping tree trunk.

'Quick! It's morning!' he yelled.

By the time Amelia stirred, Pete was standing outside looking around.

He couldn't believe his eyes. They were beside the stream… and there was the outcrop of rocks! They had slept right alongside the campsite all night!

'Where's your Dad?' Amelia asked when they stopped in front of the remains of the campfire.

'Probably looking for us,' Pete replied his breath turning to little white puffs in the crisp morning air.

He put more wood on the fire and headed for the tent. 'Stay by the fire, and I'll get us something warm to put on.'

Amelia stomped her feet on the dewy grass and blew on her hands. She jiggled the half filled billy-can, and had just moved it over the heat when she heard her mother's voice somewhere nearby.

'Am-m-m-e-l-l-l-i-a!'

Then another voice, 'P-e-e-t-e!'

'Here! We're here! At the campsite!' Amelia screamed, turning around in a circle.

Pete rushed from the tent, his head swivelling in all directions.

Suddenly, two bedraggled figures burst out of the forest. Amelia's mother ran to her daughter, laughing and crying all at once. Pete's father beamed a tired but relieved smile as he hugged his son.

They all warmed themselves around the fire as Pete and Amelia talked about their frightening night in the forest.

'Thank you so much for taking care of my daughter, Pete,' Amelia's mother said, her hands around a steaming cup of tea.

'No problem,' Pete said. 'She was pretty brave… for a girl.'

Amelia opened her mouth, and was just about to say how she had found Pete terrified and cringing on the ground, but decided against it. He would probably get embarrassed.

'What were you going to say, Amelia?' Pete's father asked.

'Oh… just that I thought Pete was pretty caring and confident… for a boy.'

Showing Confidence

Answer the questions below about the story *Close Call.*

How did Pete and Amelia display confidence in the story?

_____

_____

_____

_____

What did Pete and Amelia do to get warm?

_____

_____

_____

_____

Instead of walking further away, what did Pete think he should do?

_____

_____

_____

_____

What may be a good thing to do if you become lost?

_____

_____

_____

_____

Survey

Survey ten students in your class about the value 'confidence'.
Graph your findings on the Survey Results sheet.

Questions	Yes	No	Unsure
1. Have you ever felt nervous or anxious?			
2. When you feel confident about something, does it give you a good feeling?			
3. Have you ever helped a person to feel more confident about something?			
4. Think of a time when someone boosted your confidence level. Did their effort improve your situation?			

Survey Results

On the pie charts below, graph the results for each question from your survey.

Question 1

Question 2

Question 3

Question 4

I Feel Confident

Search newspapers and magazines for stories that illustrate examples of confidence. Design a class 'I feel confident' notice-board for display, or write your own confidence article in the space below.

Signals and Strategies

What signals does your body give you when you are feeling anxious or nervous?

_____

_____

_____

_____

What strategies do you use to overcome your feelings of nervousness or anxiety?
Tick the ones you use:

☐ A counting or breathing technique

☐ Exercise

☐ Positive self-talk

☐ Listening to uplifting music

☐ Talking to someone about the issue

☐ Relaxing muscles

What other strategies could you use? Create a Personal Confidence Boosting Card to be used in times of distress, by listing five things that work for you.

My Confidence Boosting Tips

1. _____

2. _____

3. _____

4. _____

5. _____

Cut out and glue onto a card to carry with you or tuck inside your pencil case.

Decorate and laminate it if possible.

Objectives

▸ To help students identify the different forms that respect may take.

▸ To help students identify the importance of respect and associated behaviours, in an attempt to promote a sense of belonging and a sense of safety.

Factors Enhancing Resilience

▸ Promoting a sense of belonging and fitting in.

▸ Recognition of a special gift or talent.

▸ Promoting proactive problem-solving.

▸ Encouraging an optimistic sense of future.

Introduction to the Focus Value

As a class, or in small groups, brainstorm a definition of the focus value, 'respect'. The students may wish to refer to a dictionary or thesaurus.

Ask the students to discuss how respect can be shown at school. Ask them to list some of the behaviours that support the value of respect.

The Story: Golden Triangle

The story may be read to the students by the class teacher, or in small groups if multiple copies have been made.

Follow the story with a class discussion. Some suggested questions are:

▸ What did Jamil and Andrew spend lots of time making?

▸ Who did the boys ask for help when they had problems?

▸ What club did the boys belong to? Why was it a good idea to belong to this club?

▸ Anthony was jealous of Jamil and Andrew's boat. How did he show a lack of respect towards their hard work?

▸ Jonathon had second thoughts about what Anthony was going to do. Why?

▸ How did Andrew and Jamil feel when they found their boat destroyed?

▸ What happened in Anthony's family that made him feel disrespectful toward Andrew and Jamil's boat? Is this any reason to destroy other people's property?

▸ Jamil and Andrew respected Anthony's position and overcame their anger by doing what?

▸ How did the boys learn about respect in the story?

Materials

▸ Respect for Others activity sheet.

▸ Respect for the Environment activity sheet.

▸ Respect for Property activity sheet.

▸ Interview activity sheet.

▸ Coloured pens.

Golden Triangle

The TRIANGLE

Written by Amanda Markin
Illustrated by Ian Moule

Chapter 1

Jamil was on his belly, crawling commando-style through the long grass. He jumped up and made a run for the wood, weaving back and forth to confuse the enemy.

'Stop!' Andrew shouted, chasing after him. 'There is no escape. Give yourself up right now. We have you surrounded!'

Jamil threw himself to the ground and crawled to the makeshift raft. They had built it earlier that morning by tying large, plastic containers together with rope and attaching planks of wood in a row on top. He dragged the raft down to the water and heaved it into the stream. Quietly, he pushed it out a little deeper, climbed on board, and paddled furiously with his plastic cricket bat.

'You're a sitting duck now!' yelled Andrew, as he leapt out of the bushes and jumped from the bank onto the raft. Slowly, they sank to the bottom of the stream together. Not one of their rafts had ever stayed afloat long enough for them to row anywhere, and today was the same.

'This game is stupid. How can we ever be sailors and pirates without a ship to sail?' complained Jamil, walking off in the direction of home.

'Don't go, Jamil. We could tell my dad. He might be able to help us,' suggested Andrew, hurrying to catch up with him. They didn't have far to go because they lived across the road from some fields with the stream running through it.

Mr Abernathy was busy mowing the lawn. When he saw the dismayed look on the boys' faces, he turned the mower off and called them over. 'What seems to be the trouble, kids?' he asked.

'It's the dumb raft, Dad. It just won't sail, no matter how hard we try. Can you help us to make a proper one that will work? Please Dad,' pleaded Andrew.

'Very well. Bring all the materials to my shed and we'll see what we can do,' replied Mr Abernathy, smiling kindly at them.

Chapter 2

Building a raft was very noisy business, with lots of banging, hammering and sawing. Finally, the only thing left to do was to paint it.

'I want to paint it glossy red,' said Andrew.

'No way!' cried Jamil. 'It has to be bright blue to match the sea.'

'Why don't you paint it red with a big blue stripe on the side?' suggested Mr Abernathy.

The boys worked hard swishing the paint around, and occasionally they dabbed at each other for a joke. As they stood back to admire their work, they laughed, because they had red and blue paint all over them.

'Oh man! This is the best raft in the whole world!' exclaimed Andrew enthusiastically. 'You are the best dad ever. Thanks.'

'I can't wait to put it in the water. Can we sail it now Mr Abernathy? Can we? Can we?' asked Jamil excitedly.

'Steady on, you two. The paint won't be dry until tomorrow, so you will have to wait until then,' replied Mr Abernathy as he shut the shed door to keep the cat from jumping onto the freshly painted raft.

Both boys belonged to the life-saving club's Nippers group and had training that afternoon. At the club, all they could talk about was the new raft they had made.

'You should see it, guys. It's much better than any of the rubber rafts we have here at Nippers,' Jamil boasted.

'Yeah, it's the best one I've ever seen. I can't wait until tomorrow when we sail it. My dad says we'll be able to row for miles,' gushed Andrew, feeling very proud indeed.

'Put a sock in it will you. We don't care about your silly boat. Now get lost, both of you. We've got better things to do than listen to you two go on,' jeered Anthony, another member of the Nippers group, as he ran up the beach with a group of his mates following. They sat in a huddle, whispering and sneering.

Chapter 3

When training was over, Jamil and Andrew hurried to the carpark. They were glad that Mr Abernathy was waiting to pick them up, because they didn't want to wait with the boys who had been so mean to them.

Andrew and his dad dropped Jamil off at his house and Andrew shouted out the car window as they were leaving. 'So long, Jamil. Come over as soon as you wake up tomorrow!' Jamil was grinning as he looked back over his shoulder and gave their secret hand signal for OK.

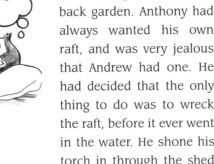

That night, Andrew was very excited and fell asleep dreaming about how he was going to be captain of his own ship, and sail the seas with Jamil as his crew.

He was in such a deep sleep that he didn't hear the rustling noises as something moved outside the house.

'Psst. I'm over here,' whispered Anthony to his friend, who was also hiding in Andrew's back garden. Anthony had always wanted his own raft, and was very jealous that Andrew had one. He had decided that the only thing to do was to wreck the raft, before it ever went in the water. He shone his torch in through the shed window and there was the prized creation. Even he had to admit it looked pretty cool; it was so shiny.

'This way! Hurry up, and be quiet will you,' Anthony ordered. They crept into the shed and stood gaping at the raft.

'Are you sure this is a good idea?' whined Jonathon, who was feeling nervous about the whole plan. Anthony ignored him. Picking up a hammer, he bashed right into the side of the beautiful raft, leaving a huge hole.

Jonathon whimpered, 'Aaah! Look what you've done! We're going to get into big trouble for this. I'm going,' he whispered and ran off.

Unfortunately, nothing was going to stop Anthony, and he smashed the poor little raft into pieces. Then he sneaked away, not noticing that his black cap had fallen off.

Chapter 4

The following morning was sunny, and Jamil washed his face and pulled his clothes on in record time. He ran to Andrew's house and knocked on the front door.

As he waited, he could hear Andrew rushing down the stairs answering his mother, 'Yes Mum, I've eaten breakfast and I've got my old clothes on. Bye. We'll be at the stream.' He opened the door and grabbed Jamil excitedly.

'This is it! Finally, we sail together. Let's go! Let's go now!' he shouted, nearly pushing Jamil over in his hurry to get to the shed.

Andrew pulled the door open and stopped dead, not believing his eyes. Their brand new raft was destroyed. Jamil could not speak; he just stood there staring. Andrew was devastated and started to cry. He ran back to the house to get his father.

Mr Abernathy came at once, even though he was still in his pyjamas.

'Do you know who could have done this?' he asked his son.

'No Dad,' replied Andrew, sniffing. As Mr Abernathy looked around the shed at the chaos, he noticed a black cap.

'Does this cap belong to either of you?' he asked as he picked it up for a closer look.

'I've never seen it before,' answered Andrew. 'Have you Jamil?'

'It's not mine,' Jamil replied, shaking his head.

'A. Picket. Isn't that the name of one of the boys at Nippers?' asked Mr Abernathy as he read the label inside the cap. 'You know the one I mean, the big lad. I think his name is Anthony. That's it, Anthony Picket.' Mr Abernathy strode off saying, 'Come on, boys. We are going to get to the bottom of this right now.'

Chapter 5

As soon as Mr Abernathy was dressed, they all jumped into the car and drove to Anthony Picket's home. Andrew and Jamil waited in the car while Mr Abernathy rang the front door bell. Mrs Picket answered, and the boys could see that she looked worried and upset. Then she closed the door.

Next, Anthony appeared in the doorway, and his face turned red with shame. 'Just look at him,' Jamil said. 'Guilty. He looks guilty. He must have done it.'

'Yeah, it was him alright,' agreed Andrew. 'I wonder if he will have to go to jail?'

When Mr Abernathy returned to the car, they couldn't have been more surprised when he said, 'Boys, I have invited Anthony to come over this afternoon to help us build another raft.' Andrew objected, 'But Dad...'

His father interrupted. 'Andrew, I will hear no more about it. I have just learned that Mr Picket was hit by a car last Wednesday, and he has been unconscious in hospital ever since. Anthony has been very upset. Even so, he understands that there is never a good reason to wreck someone else's property. He has been honest and admitted that he did it.'

'I loved that raft, Dad. It was the best!' cried Andrew with his hands on his hips.

'How do we know that Anthony won't smash the next one?' asked Jamil, glaring straight at Anthony who had come over to the car.

'I promise I won't ever do anything like that again. I was feeling angry about my dad being so sick, and I was jealous as well. I know it's no excuse, but I always wanted a raft, and I couldn't stand being left out while you and Andrew were so happy. Please forgive me and let me have a chance to make it up to you.'

The boys thought for a minute. 'Maybe we could have adventures together in the wood,' suggested Andrew. 'You are very good at rowing.' Jamil agreed. 'Yes, and he could probably help us carry all the heavy stuff we need for our games.' Mr Abernathy smiled and said, 'That settles it then.'

Mrs Picket gave her permission for Anthony to go home with them. The afternoon was busy, and they all worked very hard as Mr Abernathy supervised the building of the new raft.

It was longer and wider than the original raft, and when it was finally painted in glossy red with a blue stripe on the side, they all sat on the grass to admire it. 'Wow! It looks even better than the first one. Now all we need is a name for this little beauty,' said Andrew.

'How about Red Rover?' Jamil suggested.

'But Rover's a dog's name. What about Sea Dragon?' said Andrew.

'That's good, but what do you think about the Golden Triangle? Get it? Triangle stands for the three of us, who built the best raft in the whole world,' said Anthony.

'Yeah, that's a perfect name!' the other boys agreed. Together they painted the name in large gold letters and the raft shone like a real treasure, at least to the boys.

All that remained was to try it in the water. The next day, that's exactly what the trio did. It actually took all three of them to carry the large raft to the stream. 'Careful as you lower her in!' shouted Andrew. 'Easy now, steady as she goes.'

'Permission to board, Sir?' asked Jamil, who was about to burst with excitement as he climbed onto the raft. To their absolute amazement, the new raft remained afloat.

'Captain coming aboard!' shouted Andrew, dropping down onto the raft with his fingers crossed, hoping it would not sink. He held his breath and waited. Nothing happened. The two boys were on board, and they were still afloat.

'Cast off,' ordered Captain Andrew.

'Aye, aye Sir,' replied Anthony, as he climbed aboard and pushed the raft out into the middle of the stream. The three boys screamed with delight as they paddled madly with their plastic cricket bats, and actually sailed down the stream.

'This is the best fun ever! Three cheers for us,' they all cried out loud.

Respect for Others

What does the word 'respect' mean to you?

Why is it important to demonstrate respect for others in your classroom? How is respect demonstrated in your classroom and school grounds?

List ten different ways that you demonstrate respect.

1. _____

2. _____

3. _____

4. _____

5. _____

6. _____

7. _____

8. _____

9. _____

10. _____

Respect for the Environment

Indigenous cultures often have great understanding and respect for their environments. Why do you think this is?

_____

_____

_____

_____

_____

Create a display showing six ways that members of your school could demonstrate respect and care for your local environment. The display could be in the form of posters, computer displays, videos, photography or oral presentations.

Respect for Property

On the lines below, write about how you show respect for other people's property at school.

_____

_____

_____

_____

_____

_____

_____

_____

_____

_____

_____

_____

On the lines below, write about how you show respect for other people's property in your local community.

_____

_____

_____

_____

_____

_____

_____

_____

_____

_____

_____

_____

_____

_____

Interview

Interview an older member of your family about 'respect' and ask them how it was demonstrated when they were young.

Survey question	Comments
1. How was respect for teachers shown at school?	
2. How was respect shown towards parents?	
3. How was respect shown towards women when travelling in a bus or train?	
4. Do you think that the level of respect towards people has changed in society? Explain. How do you think the media influences the level of respect? for example, TV shows, music lyrics, reported news items.	

Discuss your findings with class members.

From your interview questions, do you think that the idea and demonstration of 'respect' has changed over the past few decades? If so, in what ways?

_____

_____

_____

_____

Objectives

▶ To help students identify the various forms that courage can take.

▶ To help students identify behaviours and values that promote a sense of belonging and a sense of safety.

Factors Enhancing Resilience

▶ Promoting a sense of fitting in or belonging.

▶ Recognising a special talent or gift.

▶ Promoting proactive problem-solving.

▶ Enhancing positive social orientation.

▶ Encouraging an optimistic sense of future.

Introduction to the Focus Value

As a class, or in small groups, brainstorm a definition of the focus value, 'courage'. The students may wish to refer to a dictionary or thesaurus.

Ask the students to discuss how courage can be shown at school. Ask them to list some of the behaviours that support the value of courage.

The Story: Jeff's Medal

The story may be read to the students by the class teacher, or in small groups if multiple copies have been made.

Follow the story with a class discussion. Some suggested questions are:

▶ What was Sam scared of?

▶ Why was she unsure about going on the camp?

▶ Why did Rebecca suggest that they ask Jeff for help?

▶ What did Jeff tell Sam about the courage of the lion from The Wizard of Oz?

▶ What do you think courage is? Where do you find it?

▶ How did Jeff overcome his fear of water?

▶ Why did Sam give Jeff a medal?

▶ When you are trying to overcome something you are scared of, what do you think is the most important thing to have? (Answers might include: to be prepared to try, believing you can do it, or having the support of friends and family.)

Materials

▶ Medal of Courage activity sheet.

▶ My Achievement activity sheet.

▶ Find the Courage activity sheet.

▶ What Courage Means to Me activity sheet.

▶ Coloured pens.

Chapter 1

Sam didn't know why she was scared of water, she just was. Probably her fear had begun when she was swept under by a wave at the beach as a toddler. Since then, she had refused to get into the bath. Instead, she had showers. Once, her mum had taken her to swimming lessons, but Sam had screamed until she was safely back on firm concrete. Somehow, Sam and water just didn't mix.

This year, Sam's class was going on a school camp. They were going to stay in Devon where they would canoe, swim and walk. Sam wanted to go, but she told her friend Rebecca that she wouldn't be going. How could she watch while the others played in the water?

Rebecca spoke to her mum about Sam's problem. She suggested they ask Rebecca's cousin, Jeff, to help. He had nearly drowned in a pool when he was five. Overcoming his fear of water, Jeff had become a swimmer and a coach.

Chapter 2

That weekend, Rebecca's mum drove Sam and Rebecca into town to visit Jeff. He showed them around his house and the back garden. Then he took them in to see the indoor pool. 'Ready for a swim, Rebecca?' Jeff asked.

'I'll watch from a safe distance,' Sam answered.

'Why don't you sit with your feet on the steps, Sam?'

'Because I'll get wet!' Sam felt an uncomfortable tightness in her chest. Sweat stood out on her forehead and she was shivering.

Rebecca looked like she belonged in the water, just like a mermaid.

'Right. Out of the pool please, Rebecca. We're all going to put on these life-saving vests. Now Rebecca, can you get back into the pool and try to go under the water?'

Rebecca tried to duck-dive. 'I can't,' she said. 'The jacket's holding me up.'

'Can you see that?' Jeff asked Sam, handing her the jacket.

'I'll put the vest on, but I know it's not going to help. And I'm not going in, anyway.' replied Sam.

Chapter 3

'Have you seen The Wizard Of Oz?' Jeff asked. 'What did the lion want?'

'He wanted some courage.'

'That's what you need! Where did the lion find his courage?'

'I can't remember… The wizard gave him a medal.'

'For a courageous act. But the lion had always had courage. He just didn't know it!' Jeff picked up a gold medallion with a blue velvet ribbon.

'I was petrified of water; I couldn't even sit beside a pool like this. I had to find my courage and take one step at a time into the water. That's what I want you to do. This was the first gold medal I won as a swimmer. Put the medal on and stand on the steps.'

'I don't think I can do it,' Sam said, feeling queasy.

'I want you to try. I want you to say to yourself, 'I can do it.''

'OK. I can do it. I can do it. I can do it…' she chanted.

Rebecca held Sam's left hand and Jeff, her right. They walked beside her to the pool steps. Sam felt dizzy, as though she might faint.

They stood still for a moment. Sam stared at Jeff, not daring to look down. 'Take a deep breath and say, 'I can do it.''

'I can do it,' Sam said as she breathed in and stepped down. The water covered her feet up to her ankles. Quickly, Jeff turned her around to face the wall rather than the pool itself.

'Fantastic! You did do it! You deserve that medal! Enough for today.'

The three of them stepped out of the water. Sam was shaking, but she also had a great big grin.

'Next week, we're going to climb down those steps.'

And the following week they did. The week after that, they walked across the pool. Then they floated on the mat.

Many weeks later, Sam fell in. She put her feet down on the bottom of the pool and stood up and laughed.

Before she went on the school camp, Sam gave Jeff a medal engraved with a picture of a lion. It was for knowing how to help her overcome her fear, and for being the best coach she could ever have.

Medal of Courage

In the space below, design a medal that you might give someone for his or her courage.

My Achievement

Write about a time when you used 'courage' to help achieve something that was important to you.

_____

_____

_____

_____

_____

_____

_____

_____

In the box below, illustrate your achievement.

Finding the Courage

List six different things you do at school that may take courage to try.

1. _____

2. _____

3. _____

4. _____

5. _____

6. _____

In the space below, create a cartoon character that demonstrates courage.

What Courage Means to Me

Complete the Y chart below.

Draw what 'courage' looks like to you.

Write what 'courage' feels like for you.

Draw what colour and shape the word 'courage' represents to you.

Objectives

▸ To help students identify the various forms that determination can take.

▸ To help students understand that sometimes we need to become determined in order to overcome a challenge or achieve a goal.

Factors Enhancing Resilience.

▸ Promoting proactive problem-solving.

▸ Enhancing positive social orientation.

▸ Encouraging an optimistic sense of future.

▸ Promoting a sense of belonging and fitting in.

Introduction to the Focus Value

As a class, or in small groups, brainstorm a definition of the focus value, 'determination'. The students may wish to refer to a dictionary or thesaurus.

Ask the students to discuss how determination can be shown at school. Ask them to list some of the behaviours that support the value of determination.

The Story: Lia's Leap

The story may be read to the students by the class teacher, or in small groups if multiple copies have been made.

Follow the story with a class discussion. Some suggested questions are:

▸ Why did Lia not want to stay at Aimee's house?

▸ Where did Lia and her family usually live?

▸ Lia decided to stay inside the whole time. Why?

▸ Why did Lia decide to get onto the trampoline?

▸ What advice would you give to Lia about her fear of hens?

▸ Do you think Lia was determined to overcome her fear of hens? Explain why.

Materials

▸ My Determination activity sheet.

▸ My Success Recipe activity sheet.

▸ The Determinations activity sheet.

▸ Using Determination activity sheet.

▸ White cardboard, pencils, glue and black cardboard for The Determinations activity.

▸ Coloured pens.

Lia's Leap

Written by Claire Saxby
Illustrated by Peta Taylor

Chapter 1

Aimee, Lia's best friend, was going on holiday.

'We're going for three whole, long weeks, and while we're on holiday,' said Aimee, 'you're going to be having a holiday at our house!' Aimee stopped and stared at Lia, who suddenly looked very pale.

'Lia. LIA! Did you hear me?'

Lia blinked. 'What do you mean?' she asked. 'It's all arranged. I heard my mum talking to your mum last night.' Aimee grabbed Lia's hands and half dragged, half skipped her around in a circle.

'You'll sleep in my bed, and there're the swings, and you'll be able to jump on my trampoline all day if you want.'

A holiday at Aimee's house? Lia shuddered. She loved Aimee's trampoline, and used to bounce on it all the time. She used to love going to Aimee's house... until they got the hens.

There were four hens, and Lia was terrified of all of them.

Chapter 2

'How can you be afraid of hens?' Lia's brother scoffed, his mouth full of toast. It was the first morning of their holiday. The cereal in Lia's bowl was hardly touched. Her brother had eaten two bowls of cereal and was munching his third piece of toast. 'They're only birds! They can't even fly properly.' He flapped around in a circle.

Lia said nothing.

Her brother went outside. Lia watched longingly through the window as he jumped and somersaulted on the trampoline. She looked around the garden. She could see all the hens. One was sitting in a hole, fluffing dirt through her feathers. Another was asleep under the orange tree, and the other two were scratching the earth near the back fence. Why did Aimee have to have hens? Why couldn't they be locked up or something?

Lia's mother had grown up on a farm. 'Isn't it great to have a garden, even if it's only for a while?' she sighed. 'Perhaps one day we'll have a house with a yard.'

Lia thought about their apartment, too high for fluttering hens; it seemed fine to her.

'Why don't you go out and play in the sunshine?' Mum continued. 'Have a jump on the trampoline. You love trampolines.'

Lia kept watching through the window. She didn't really need the trampoline. And she wasn't going into that garden while those hens were there. Never. Never!

Chapter 3

'Lia,' whispered Mum. 'Come and look at this.' Mum tiptoed closer to the window. Lia followed. Outside, Lia's little sister, Minny, was sitting on a table under a tree, sucking her thumb. On her lap was the speckledy-brown hen. Lia and Mum watched in silence.

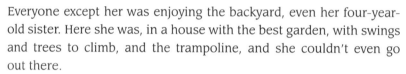

'It's amazing! Minny never sits still,' murmured Mum. 'Perhaps we'd better bring the hen in at dinnertime. Maybe then she'd sit still for dinner!' Mum laughed. 'See, Lia, there's nothing to be frightened of. The hens won't hurt you. They're as gentle as lambs.'

The lambs at the farm jumped everywhere and pushed at their bottles. That wasn't gentle.

Lia read some books. She played with Aimee's dolls. She made faces into the mirror, poking her tongue out at her grumpy reflection.

Everyone except her was enjoying the backyard, even her four-year-old sister. Here she was, in a house with the best garden, with swings and trees to climb, and the trampoline, and she couldn't even go out there.

It wasn't fair. She felt like she was in a cage at the zoo, while everyone else was outside having all the fun. There were plenty of things to do inside Aimee's house, but three weeks was a very long time to be stuck inside. Too long.

Chapter 4

Lia took a deep breath. She could feel her heart pounding. Perhaps if she was very quiet, she could more easily count the hens. One on her sister's lap. A black one and a white one were fighting over the last of the grain in the food bowl. That made three. Where was the other one?

She looked over to where her sister was sitting. Only one hen there. She looked to where Mum was reading a magazine and sipping her coffee. No hens there.

She looked to where her brother was sitting in the fork of the apple tree. No hens in the tree. Lia couldn't see the fourth hen anywhere.

Slowly, very slowly, she inched the door open. Flutter, flutter, flutter, went the noise in her ears. Boom, boom, boom, went her heart. Lia didn't look right. She didn't look left. She was determined to run straight towards the trampoline.

Then she saw the fourth hen. It had been in the shadow cast by the trampoline. Lia sprang into the air, fear giving her wings. She jumped higher than she had ever jumped before, even on a trampoline.

As she jumped, so did the hen, fluttering and squawking. The booming of Lia's heart sounded even louder. The hen scuttled away as though she'd seen a fox.

Plop! Lia landed on the bouncy black mat. She rolled over and lay there on her back, as the trampoline, and her heart, slowly settled.

She'd made it! A big grin filled her face. Lia stood up and began bouncing.

She didn't think about how she was going to get off the trampoline. That could wait. For now, she had some bouncing to catch up on.

My Determination

Prepare a short talk about yourself (lasting one minute) on the lines below. The talk should give the audience as much information as possible about a time when you needed, and used, determination to overcome an obstacle or achieve a goal.

_____

_____

_____

_____

_____

_____

_____

_____

_____

_____

_____

_____

_____

_____

Display your draft in the classroom to remind students how useful determination can be.

My Success Recipe

In the space below, write a recipe for success using determination as one of your ingredients. Use the genre of recipe writing.

The Determinations

Using text and illustrations, create a CD cover for your group The Determinations.

On the back, list your top ten songs. Paste onto cardboard. You can make the disks from black cardboard.

When completed hang the CDs around the classroom.

Using Determination

In what ways could you use determination to help you achieve your goals in areas such as:

- ▸ school subjects
- ▸ sport
- ▸ friendship challenges
- ▸ developing a special interest or hobby.

Write or draw about your ideas in the space below.

Report your ideas to your class, or share them with a friend.

Objectives

▸ To help students identify the various forms that caring can take.

▸ To help students identify behaviours and values that promote a sense of belonging and a sense of safety.

Factors Enhancing Resilience

▸ Promoting a sense of fitting in or belonging.

▸ Recognising a special talent or gift.

▸ Promoting proactive problem-solving.

▸ Enhancing positive social interaction.

▸ Encouraging an optimistic sense of future.

Introduction to the Focus Value

As a class, or in small groups, brainstorm a definition of the focus value, 'caring'. The students may wish to refer to a dictionary or thesaurus.

Ask the students to discuss how caring can be shown at school. Ask them to list some of the behaviours that support the value of caring.

The Story: Hop, Skip and Jump!

The story may be read to the students by the class teacher, or in small groups if multiple copies have been made.

Follow the story with a class discussion. Some suggested questions are:

▸ What is caring?

▸ How was caring behaviour portrayed in the story?

▸ What type of behaviours could be classified as caring behaviours?

▸ Why do people like to be caring?

Materials

▸ Caring for Others activity sheet.

▸ Survey activity sheet.

▸ Survey Results activity sheet.

▸ Stories about Caring activity sheet.

▸ Newspapers and magazines.

Hop, Skip and Jump!

Written by Claire Saxby
Illustrated by Katie Jardine

Chapter 1

'Come and skip with me, Gran,' said Tina.

'Oh, I wish I could!' replied Gran. 'When I was young, I skipped all the time, and when I wasn't skipping, I was hopping or jumping. But I think I've used up all my hops, skips and jumps. I don't seem to have any left.'

Tina hopped down the hall, skipped with her skipping rope and jumped up and down the stairs. Then she sat down to think.

If Gran had used up all her hops, skips and jumps, would that happen to Tina too? Would she run out of jumps, skips or hops? How many did each person get? Did some people get more than others?

Mum was always saying that Tina should slow down and walk sometimes, just so she didn't forget how. Did that mean she was using up her skips too fast and would run out of them?

How many skips had she skipped today? How many times had she jumped? How many hops had she done? Perhaps she'd run out soon.

This was terrible. Tina tried to imagine life without skips or jumps or hops. She couldn't. Poor Gran. Tina felt like crying.

Chapter 2

'What's the matter, Tina?' It was Gran. She sat down on the step next to Tina.

'It's my skips,' said Tina. 'I don't want to run out of them like you did.'

Gran gave her a hug. 'I'm sorry,' she said. 'I didn't mean it quite like that, and I didn't mean to make you sad.'

She hugged Tina again.

'I didn't really lose them; I was just so busy

looking after your mum and her brothers, that there didn't seem to be any time for skipping. And my old joints don't move as easily as they used to.'

Chapter 3

In bed that night, Tina dreamed that she couldn't hop, skip or jump, but everyone else in her dream could. They hopped, skipped and jumped across the park. They hopped, skipped and jumped down the street. They hopped, skipped and jumped up and down the supermarket aisles. Teachers in school hopped, skipped and jumped around the front of the classroom. Even women with white hair, and men with beards down to their toes, hopped, skipped and jumped in her dream.

Sometimes they made noises like rusty hinges. When that happened, a girl in overalls would tip some oil on their joints and off they'd go again. But all Tina could do was watch. Maybe that was what it was like for Gran.

There had to be a way to get Gran some more hops, skips and jumps.

Chapter 4

'C'mon Gran,' she said next morning.

'Where are we going?' asked Gran.

'Outside,' said Tina. She held out her hand to Gran.

'What are we doing?' asked Gran.

'I'm going to find you some skips. Maybe they're not gone, just lost... and if we can't find yours, you can have some of mine.'

'That's very caring of you, Tina, to share your skips with me,' replied her gran lovingly.

It would be worth a thousand skips to see Gran skip again, Tina thought.

'Watch me,' said Tina.

Gran watched. 'I'm not sure…' she said.

Tina took Gran's hand. They skipped together. Just a few little skips, but they were proper skips. Gran let go of Tina's hand.

'Have you had enough, Gran?'

'No, I'm just checking…' she said, laughing. 'You found my skips, perhaps I'd better check my hops and jumps too!'

Tina and her gran laughed happily together.

Caring for Others

Answer the questions below about the story, Hop, Skip and Jump!

After she had finished skipping, what did Tina sit down to think about?

_____

_____

_____

Why did Tina feel like crying?

_____

_____

_____

Why was it so important for Tina to find her gran's skips?

_____

_____

_____

How did Gran find her skips again?

_____

_____

_____

Survey

Survey ten students in your class about the value of caring. Graph your findings on the Survey Results sheet.

Question	Yes	No	Unsure
1. Have you ever acted in a caring way toward someone?			
2. When you were caring, did it give you a good feeling?			
3. Did your act of caring help the other person?			
4. Think of a time when someone was caring to you. Did their caring help your situation?			

Survey Results

Graph your results for each question on the pie charts below.

Question 1

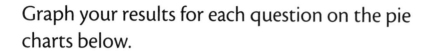

Question 2

Question 3

Question 4

Stories About Caring

Search newspapers and magazines for stories that illustrate caring.

Design a class notice-board for a display of these stories, or write a summary in the space below about the caring example you have found.

Our Play About Caring

In a small group, create a short play about an example of 'caring'. It could be a scene that happens:

- at school
- at home
- in sport
- from a fairy tale
- from a newspaper article
- from a news item
- from a real story.

In your play, you need to include a problem for a member of the group that is overcome by the caring efforts of others.

Notes:

_____

_____

_____

_____

_____

_____

_____

_____

_____

_____

_____

_____

Objectives

▸ To help students identify different lifestyles and how these may differ between families.

▸ For students to examine roles and responsibilities.

Factors Enhancing Resilience

▸ Promoting a sense of fitting in or belonging.

▸ Recognising a special talent or gift.

▸ Promoting proactive problem-solving.

▸ Enhancing positive social orientation.

▸ Encouraging an optimistic sense of future.

Introduction to the Focus Value

As a class, or in small groups, brainstorm a definition of the focus value, 'assertiveness'. The students may wish to refer to a dictionary or thesaurus.

Ask the students to discuss how assertiveness can be shown at school. Ask them to list some of the behaviours that support the value of assertiveness.

The Story: Just For Once

The story may be read to the students by the class teacher, or in small groups if multiple copies have been made.

Follow the story with a class discussion. Some suggested questions are:

▸ How did Miguel feel when he started at his new school? Why?

▸ What did Miguel do, even though he wished he could talk about his holidays?

▸ Miss Moore asked for someone in the class to tell about their mother's or father's job. What did Miguel do?

▸ Jonathon put his hand up for everything. Do you think it is more important to get something right, or to try?

▸ Even though Miguel knew the missing word, why do you think he didn't put up his hand?

▸ How do you feel when you know you are good at something?

Materials

▸ Interview activity sheet.

▸ All About Me activity sheet.

▸ Being Assertive activity sheet.

▸ What I'd Like To Do activity sheet.

Just For Once

Written by Helen Miles
Illustrated by Katie Jardine

Chapter 1

Miguel's parents looked for work after setting up their new home in England, and soon Miguel started at his new school.

'I like my teacher, and most of the kids are OK,' he told his mother in Spanish. 'But I wish I could learn the language quicker. I feel so dumb!'

'Well, perhaps if we speak only in English at home, we will all improve,' his mother said.

Miguel nodded, but teaching his brain to think in English, not Spanish, was proving to be harder than he had thought.

Chapter 2

'Who would like to read aloud?' Miss Moore asked the class the next morning.

Five hands shot up in the air. But Miguel kept his on the desk.

Miss Moore chose Freya. Everyone knew she was good at reading.

'This story is about a beautiful princess who saves a prince from a fire-breathing dragon,' Freya began.

That was a funny story, Miguel thought when Freya finished. Especially the part about the princess ordering the dragon to 'sit'. But, just for once, I wish I could read a story without making a mistake.

Chapter 3

'Now, who would like to talk about their holidays?' asked Miss Moore.

Four hands shot up in the air. Again, Miguel kept his on the desk.

Miss Moore chose Roberto. Everyone knew he spoke very well.

'We spent our holidays on a sheep farm in Australia...' Roberto began.

His holiday sounded like fun, Miguel thought. Especially the part about helping to shear the sheep. But, just for once, I wish I could talk about my holidays when I lived in Spain.

Chapter 4

'Who would like to tell the class about their mother's or father's job?' asked Miss Moore. Three hands shot up in the air, but Miguel still kept his on the desk.

Miss Moore chose Helena. Everyone knew she was very proud of her mother.

My mother puts out fires...' she started.

That sounds like an important job, Miguel thought as Helena continued. Especially the part about her mother saving two boys from a burning building.

But, just for once, I wish I could talk about my padre who was a famous Matador in Spain.

Chapter 5

After lunch, when all the students were back in class, Miss Moore wrote a question on the blackboard: What do all the (........) in the class have in common?

'Who would like to fill in the missing word?' she asked.

Two hands shot up in the air.

As before, Miguel kept his on his desk.

Miss Moore chose Jonathan.

Everyone knew he put his hand up for everything. He wrote in the word 'childrin'.

I was right, thought Miguel. But, just for once, I wish I could have filled in the missing word.

'Right word, Jonathan, but wrong spelling,' Miss Moore said. She changed the spelling to 'children'.

'Now, who would like to come up and illustrate the sentence?' she asked.

One hand left the desk and shot up in the air very assertively.

Miss Moore nodded at Miguel. Everyone knew he was good at drawing. He drew five different children, but they all had two things in common. They had their hands in the air and they were smiling.

'Very good, Miguel. Everyone in the class gets a chance to put their hand up,' Miss Moore said. 'And Miguel, just for once, I wish I could draw like you.'

Interview

Choose ten students from your class and list their names below.
Interview them about a time in their lives when they were
assertive.

Name	Example of being assertive
1.	
2.	
3.	
4.	
5.	
6.	
7.	
8.	
9.	
10.	

All About Me

Prepare a short talk about yourself, lasting one minute.

The talk should give the audience as much information about yourself as possible in the time given. You could mention family, pets, holidays, favourite food, hobbies and hopes for the future. Include an example of a time in your life when you were assertive.

_____

_____

_____

_____

_____

_____

_____

_____

_____

_____

_____

_____

_____

_____

_____

_____

The class can vote on the class member who presented the most information to the class in the one minute, and gave a good example of assertiveness in their talk.

Being Assertive

In the space below, list three behaviours that people use when they are assertive.

Assertive behaviours

1. _____

2. _____

3. _____

How do you think that learning to be assertive may help you at school and later in life?

_____

_____

_____

_____

_____

_____

_____

_____

What I'd Like To Do

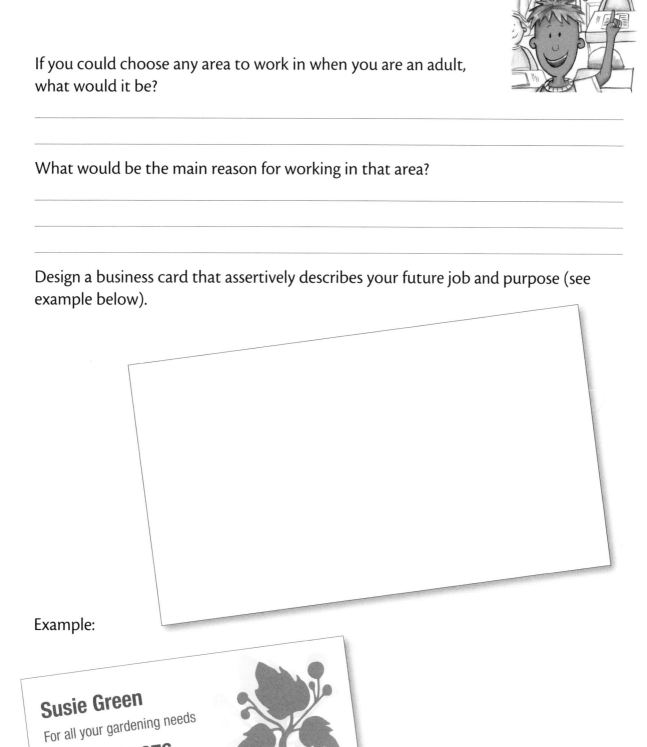

If you could choose any area to work in when you are an adult, what would it be?

_____

_____

What would be the main reason for working in that area?

_____

_____

_____

Design a business card that assertively describes your future job and purpose (see example below).

Example:

Susie Green
For all your gardening needs
1800 624 9876
No job too small

'Let's Green the environment for a better world!'

Benard, B. (1995) *Fostering Resiliency in Kids: Protective Factors in the Family, School and Community,* Western Centre for Drug Free Schools and Communities, Portland, Oregon.

Cahill, H. (1999) Why a Whole-school Approach to Enhancing Resilience?, *Mindmatters Newsletter,* March, p 2.

Canfield, J. and Siccone, F. (1995) *101 Ways to Develop Student Self-esteem and Responsibility,* Massachussetts: Allyn and Bacon.

Cantor, R., Kivel, P. and Creighton, A. (1997) *Days of Respect:* Organising a School-wide Violence Prevention Programme, Hunter House, California.

Catalano, R. and Hawkins, J.D. (Ed) 'The social development model: a theory of antisocial behaviour'. In Hawkins J.D. (Ed) *Delinquency and Crime: Current Theories,* New York, Cambridge Publications.

Centre for Adolescent Health (1998) *The Gatehouse Project: Promoting Emotional Well-being: A Whole-school Approach – Team Guidelines,* Centre for Adolescent Health, Melbourne.

Department of Education, Victoria (1999) *Framework for Student Services in Victorian Schools:* Teacher resource, Department of Education, Victoria.

DfES (2003) *Developing children's social, emotional and behavioural skills:* a whole curriculum approach. Primary National Strategy.

Fuller, A. (2001). Background Paper on Resilience presented to the Northern Territory Principal's Association (Australia).

Fuller, A., McGraw, K. and Goodyear, M. (1998) *The Mind of Youth.* Department of Education, Melbourne, Australia.

Fuller, A. (1998) *From Surviving to Thriving: Promoting Mental Health in Young People,* ACER Press, Melbourne.

Goleman, D. (1995) *Emotional Intelligence – Why it matters more than IQ,* Bloomsbury, London.

Hawkins, J. and Catalano, R. (1993) *Communities that Care:* Risk and Protective Focused Prevention Using the Social Development Strategy, Developmental Research and Programmes Incorporated, Seattle, USA.

Lickona, T. (1997) *'Educating for Character: a comprehensive approach'* in Molnar (ed.) The Construction of Children's Character, University of Chicago Press, Chicago.

Olweus, D. (1995) *Bullying or Peer Abuse at School –* facts and interventions. Current Directions in Psychological Science, 4,6, p 196-200.

Resnick, M.D., Harris, L.J. and Blum, R.W. (1993) *The impact of caring and connectedness on adolescent health and wellbeing,* Journal of Paediatrics and Child Health, 29.

Rigby, K. (1996) *Bullying in schools and what we can do about it.* ACER Press, Melbourne, Australia.

Seligman, M. (1995) *The Optimistic Child.* NSW: Random House, Australia.

Smith, C. and McKee, S. (2005) *Becoming an Emotionally Healthy School.* A Lucky Duck Book, Paul Chapman, London.

Taylor, M. (2000) *'Values Education: Issues and challenges in policy and school practice'* in M. Leicester, C. Modgil and S. Modgil (ed.), Education, Culture and Values, Vol 2, Falmer Press, London.